Sixty Years On –
Who Cares for the NHS?

T0170252

Sixty Years On –
Who Cares for the NHS?

HELEN EVANS

The Institute of Economic Affairs

First published in Great Britain in 2008 by
The Institute of Economic Affairs
2 Lord North Street
Westminster
London sw1p 3lb
in association with Profile Books Ltd

The mission of the Institute of Economic Affairs is to improve public understanding of the fundamental institutions of a free society, by analysing and expounding the role of markets in solving economic and social problems.

A CIP catalogue record for this book is available from the British Library.

isbn 978 0 255 36611 3

Many IEA publications are translated into languages other than English or are reprinted. Permission to translate or to reprint should be sought from the Director General at the address above.

Typeset in Stone by MacGuru Ltd
info@macguru.org.uk

Printed and bound in Great Britain by Hobbs the Printers

To Tim and Petica

CONTENTS

THE AUTHOR

Dr Helen Evans is a health policy expert and a registered nurse with a wealth of clinical and healthcare delivery experience. She is currently director of Nurses for Reform, a Health Fellow with the Adam Smith Institute, and a director of the leading predictive public affairs consultancy Farsight SPI.

A former university guest lecturer and graduate in health management, she has extensive knowledge of British and European health policy and, in 2006, obtained her PhD in Health Economics from Brunel University.

Helen has worked for a range of think tanks, including the Centre for New Europe in Brussels. Her nursing career has seen her work as a senior nurse in the Royal London Hospitals Trust and St Bartholomew's Hospital.

FOREWORD

This publication, released to mark the 60th anniversary of the National Health Service, puts before readers important research that highlights the extent to which key players in opinion-forming circles no longer believe in nationalised healthcare.

As such, it provides a snapshot of the judgements and attitudes of key opinion formers on a state healthcare system that was not only built in an era of command and control but which beds into its very fabric the privileges of professional monopoly power.

Following the Labour government's welcome embrace of the independent sector as providers of healthcare, and its increasing emphasis – in theory if not in practice – on patient choice, perhaps there should be little surprise that such opinion formers now consider a wide range of statist restrictions in healthcare with increased suspicion.

Should the state own hospitals? Why shouldn't GPs, doctors, nurses and indeed all healthcare providers be free to advertise and build – from the bottom up – trusted healthcare brands? Why should the state enforce censorship of information about healthcare? Why should providers not be faced with the demands of informed consumers? Moreover, is it right that the state should privilege medical and health professionals with monopoly legislative favour, as they now enjoy with the General Medical Council and the Nursing and Midwifery Council?

Ultimately, why cannot consumers and the poorest in society benefit from open competition in healthcare, and thus see a profound redistribution of power?

At the 60th anniversary of the NHS, the ways in which opinion formers react to these and other key questions will be of crucial importance for the future. It is in this context that I commend this publication and the significant research findings that it presents.

STEPHEN POLLARD
President, Centre for the New Europe
May 2008

The views expressed in this monograph are, as in all IEA publications, those of the author and not those of the Institute (which has no corporate view), its managing trustees, Academic Advisory Council members or senior staff.

ACKNOWLEDGEMENTS

It would be impossible to fully acknowledge and thank all the people who have supported me during the research and writing of this project. Not only is their number great but given the sensitivity of the subject many have chosen to remain anonymous. Of those who can be highlighted, a special mention must go to Professor David Marsland of Brunel University. I must also mention Dr Chris R. Tame, the founder of the Libertarian Alliance, who even in the last few weeks of his terminal illness continued to encourage me with my work. I wish also to thank my husband and mentor Dr Tim Evans, without whom I would never have undertaken this project. Needless to say, any omissions or errors remain entirely my responsibility.

SUMMARY

- The consensus that lay behind the concept of a centrally planned, government-funded National Health Service is now broken.
- The market alternative to the UK's National Health Service is not a US-style system. The US system is planned, regulated and government funded to a very high degree.
- Many academics and policy experts analyse health policy in the neoclassical 'market-failure' paradigm. The idea of a perfect market is postulated as an ideal, ways in which a market in health might fall short of this are identified, and government action is proposed to remedy the shortcomings.
- The market-failure paradigm is wrong. It assumes that government can behave with perfect foresight to correct apparent failings in a health market. Instead, we must rationally explore whether a market in health or government planning provides the better outcomes.
- A major new survey of elite opinion in this monograph shows that the shortcomings with government-planned healthcare are well recognised among all opinion-forming groups. Academics, think tank policy experts and policy advisers appear to have the greatest scepticism about government healthcare provision and the greatest confidence in the market. Politicians seem to have greater confidence in the political process to provide effective healthcare.

- Opinion formers now consider the problem of monopoly and lack of consumer information to be substantially greater problems in a government-provided healthcare system than they would be in a market-based system of healthcare.
- Opinion formers believe that, if there were a market in healthcare, government would need to step in to fill in the gaps because some people would not get adequate provision. They believe almost as strongly, however, that the state 'cannot do it all' and that the private sector and charities need to supplement state health provision.
- Elite opinion's view of the role of the state and the market very much reflects the neoclassical health economics model. There is relatively little confidence in centrally planning a service solely provided by the state; the private sector is welcomed; but notions of 'market failure' seem to dominate thinking about the limitations of markets.
- It is significant that the most pro-market views are those expressed by academics, think tank experts and policy advisers. Such people can often be a leading indicator of general opinion many years ahead. Although elite opinion has moved only so far to date, specific groups of elite opinion are beginning to push the boundaries of discourse farther.
- Part of the vision of a free market in healthcare will involve government removing the privileges it has given to professional groups to exclude non-members from the practice of medicine. A highly regulated market, ridden with statutory monopolies, is not a free market at all. This is one important respect in which the boundaries of the healthcare debate must be pushed farther if markets are going to replace state provision.

TABLES

**Sixty Years On –
Who Cares for the NHS?**

1 INTRODUCTION

This monograph explores one of the most important issues concerning people around the world today: the organisation and delivery of healthcare. Analysing the opinions of an influential range of British health opinion formers, it seeks to question and explore the dominant paradigm of market failure in mainstream health economics. Moreover, in seeking to clarify and examine commonly held notions of market failure among a sample of key health opinion formers including professionals, politicians and journalists, it highlights the intellectual and conceptual environment in which the wider health policy conversation is popularly cited and bound.

Questioning the state's role in healthcare

Following the supply-side revolution of the 1980s, a small but growing number of academics, politicians and other opinion formers are increasingly citing government failure, rather than markets, as the enemy of better healthcare. This is true not just in countries with state monopoly healthcare provision (such as the UK) but also in countries where provision is ostensibly private but, to a large degree, controlled by the state (such as the USA). Libertarian writers such as David Friedman[1] and Brian

---

1   David D. Friedman, *The Machinery of Freedom: A Guide to Radical Capitalism*, Open Court Publishing, Chicago, 1989.

Micklethwait[2] argue that objectively there is no such thing as market failure in healthcare. Instead, many of the problems popularly blamed on the market are invariably the result of various forms of state intervention.

In Britain, as in many other developed countries around the world, the healthcare debate ultimately takes two popular forms. One opinion views state healthcare, in the British case the National Health Service, and the idea of healthcare being free at the point of delivery, as being a sacred non-negotiable principle. This perspective is portrayed by Micklethwait in the following terms:

> That people should be left to die for the mere lack of a few thousand quid for some machine that will mimic one of their organs is an abomination. We are falling behind our continental rivals, who spend a far higher proportion of their GNP on medical care. Public opinion has again and again revealed itself eager for more health care spending, and content to pay more in taxation to finance such increases. The idea of turning the whole show over to those overpriced peacocks in the medical private sector is appalling, not to say a recipe for the American health method, which is that if you get sick, you are either bankrupted or you die.[3]

The second form of popular opinion asserts that the National Health Service is simply another nationalised industry and that it has all the characteristic failures of such an organisation. Here, this school of thought can be summarised in the following terms:

> Price anything at zero (or thereabout), and the queue for it

2   Brian Micklethwait, *How and How Not to Demonopolise Medicine*, Political Notes 56, Libertarian Alliance, London, 1991.

3   Ibid., p. 1.

will stretch out infinitely. Give a succession of blank cheques to any organisation and the people running the thing will tend to abscond with or waste most of the money, even as they complain about the stinginess of the cheque signers. However, the British public being so incomprehensively wedded to the NHS, and so infuriatingly unimpressed by the medical private sector, they must not be told point blank and to their faces that the NHS ought to be closed down. No, one must be 'realistic'. One must instead speak of 'reforming' the NHS, and of making it less wasteful and better managed.[4]

For classical liberals and libertarians alike the truth lies far beyond both of these positions. The root of the problem is that in Britain and elsewhere around the world *all* medicine – state and private – is ultimately underpinned by government-sponsored monopolies. In Britain the medical monopoly resides with the General Medical Council (GMC):

If you are not or are no longer a 'doctor' (as the government, advised by its preferred bunch of doctors, understands that word), then there are three things you may not do. These are, in ascending order of importance: sign death certificates, prescribe drugs, and (in general) take medical risks ... In other words, medicine is a government sponsored monopoly. You can't practise medicine in any significant way if you can only prescribe insignificant drugs or cures, and only take insignificant risks. So far as I can judge it, things are approximately like this everywhere. In no country on earth is medicine un-interfered with by the local state.[5]

---

4   Ibid.
5   Ibid., p. 2.

The myth of the US 'market in healthcare'

In Britain and elsewhere in Europe, the USA is often seen as representing the most extreme example of a free market in healthcare. Yet in reality, there is little – if any – widespread understanding of the existence of Medicaid or Medicare, the two US state healthcare systems. Today, most British people find it hard to believe that the US government has any major state healthcare programmes, let alone that it historically spent a higher proportion of its national income on them than the British government has on the NHS.[6]

However, the USA does have large state healthcare programmes; it does spend a substantial proportion of its national income on them; and it is arguably even more restrictive when it comes to medical risks and safety than virtually anywhere else in the world:

> There, under the influence of a deranged generation of lawyers whose aim seems to be to bring civilisation itself to a standstill, *nobody* is now allowed to take medical risks, *not even doctors.* If anything goes wrong with *any* medical procedure, then no matter how conscientiously the risks were explained to the patient and no matter how many forms he signed saying that yes he understood this and please could they get on with the operation, if things then go at all badly wrong, the patient – or if he dies his relatives – can then sue the doctor for double the doctor's life savings. To spell this out in plain English, what the American lawyers are engaged in doing is *making medicine illegal. All* medicine, even medicine practised by the one government favoured American trade union. Add this obsession with safety to the fact that the American Medical Association has the same armlock on American medicine as the GMC has here, and it

---

6   David Green, *Challenge to the NHS. A Study of Competition in American Health Care and the Lessons for Britain,* Institute of Economic Affairs, London, 1989.

is hardly to be wondered at if American medical services are cripplingly expensive, and are becoming more so.[7]

To libertarians, popular debate concerning the ownership of hospitals and health funding schemes is important but only a part of an even bigger picture. The key issue is who is allowed to define, practise and therefore control medicine:

> In a free medical market, the very process of defining *who is and who is not a doctor would be negotiated entirely between the people offering themselves as doctors and the people deciding whether to submit themselves to these doctors as patients* … At the heart of the medical issue is the right of the individual to take whatever risks he wants to take and make deals on that basis, and the duty of any court, lawyers and politicians to respect rather than retrospectively overturn these details.[8]

For libertarians a genuine free market in healthcare would mean that people would be able to take whatever drugs they wanted and medical practitioners would be able to advertise their services. Over time a new consumer-driven market reliant upon reputation – not state regulation – would emerge.

> Far from being obvious to me that a truly free medical market would be disastrous, I believe on the contrary that such arrangements would be of huge benefit to mankind, and that the sooner medicine is done this way the better.
>
> Things would not, inevitably, be perfect. Some fools would make crass blunders, by ignoring manifestly superior medical services for the most frivolous of reasons, and by patronising the most notoriously incompetent. Some such fools would perish from their foolishness. Others would

---

7   Micklethwait, op. cit., p. 2.
8   Ibid.

merely be unlucky. No law can prevent either stupidity or bad luck, although the world is now filled with the particular stupidity which consists of refusing to face this truth, and with the many luckless victims of this stupidity.[9]

For Micklethwait quality and efficiency would be better driven by a consumer-led market than any centralising regime with its inherent restrictions:

> Given that for most people the avoidance of suicide rather than suicide is the objective, a truly free medical market would enable them, for the first time ever, to purchase steadily improving medical advice and medical help, and at a steadily diminishing price.
>
> One of the most pernicious restrictions on medicine imposed by the current medical regime is the restriction on advertising. In a free market rival medical procedures, rival medical 'philosophies', rival views on the relative importance of confidentiality, hygiene, speed of treatment, riskiness of treatment, and so forth, would all battle it out in the market place. 'Alternative' therapists would be allowed to prescribe potentially dangerous drugs, as only government favoured therapists may now. It would be up to the patients to pick therapists who seemed to know what they were doing and their look out if they chose badly. The already thriving medical periodical press would assist with voluminous comparative advice, praise and criticism.
>
> In such a free market, any number of different medical styles could be practised, and patients would make their choices.[10]

While libertarian authors offer a radical and powerful critique

---

9   Ibid., p. 3.
10   Ibid.

of state failure, a growing number of mainstream commentators seem to have begun a journey in this direction, citing government regulation and interference in healthcare as being against both the public and even professional interest. This study is primarily concerned with how healthcare opinion formers think about health economics at the beginning of the 21st century and more specifically at the time of the 60th anniversary of the NHS. How, for instance, do British healthcare opinion formers think about such notions as monopoly versus choice, regulation versus reputation and commercial free speech (advertising) versus health information censorship? It is to these and other key questions that this study and its core research now turns.

2 THE HISTORIC FAILURE OF THE NATIONAL HEALTH SERVICE

Early promise of the NHS

The idea of a free health service for all was first suggested in Britain by Beatrice Webb in 1909.[1] It fell, however, to Sir William Beveridge to fully articulate such a plan and to lay the foundations for the service in his 1942 paper *Social Insurance and Allied Services*.[2]

In February 1941 the Trades Union Congress had lobbied the government about the chaotic and often contradictory array of state sickness benefits that were on offer to workers. As a result, an interdepartmental committee was proposed to Cabinet and Bevin subsequently offered its chairmanship to Beveridge. On initial inspection, the terms of reference for this group sounded modest: 'To undertake, with special reference to the inter-relation of the schemes, a survey of the existing national schemes of social insurance and allied services, including workmen's compensation, and to make recommendations.'[3]

The Home Office and officials at the Ministry of Health, however, had higher hopes of a much broader examination. While

---

1   Nicholas Timmins, *The Five Giants: A Biography of the Welfare State*, HarperCollins, London, 2001, p. 15.

2   *Social Insurance and Allied Services*, Report by Sir William Beveridge, HMSO, London, 1942.

3   Timmins, op. cit., p. 18.

the Treasury wanted the committee to essentially provide a limited 'tidying up operation', Beveridge was eager to produce a visionary study that was much broader in its scope and recommendations.

In all, 127 pieces of written evidence were to be received and more than fifty private evidence sessions held with witnesses.[4] But only one piece of written evidence had arrived by December 1941 when Beveridge circulated a paper entitled 'Heads of a Scheme' which contained the essence of the final report set to appear a year later. The initial paper opened with the key statement that was to stretch the original terms of reference up to and in some ways beyond their limit:

> 1. No satisfactory scheme for social security can be devised [without the] following assumptions.
>
> A. A national health service for prevention and comprehensive treatment available to all members of the community.
>
> B. Universal children's allowances for all children up to 14 or if in full-time education up to 16.
>
> C. Full use of powers of the state to maintain employment and to reduce unemployment to seasonal, cyclical and interval unemployment, that is to say to unemployment suitable for treatment by cash allowances.[5]

Work on the committee proceeded at a pace during 1942 as witnesses were called and evidence taken.

When the report was finally published on 1 December 1942

---

4   Ibid., p. 20.
5   Much of this paper was reproduced in D. Fraser, *The Evolution of the British Welfare State*, Macmillan, London, 1973, p. 265.

it received a rapturous reception. On the night before its release there were queues to buy it outside His Majesty's Stationery Office. The first 60,000 copies sold rapidly. And sales topped more than 100,000 within a month. By the end of 1944 more than 200,000 copies had been purchased. In many ways, what made its reputation and facilitated its impact was a twenty-page introduction and a twenty-page conclusion sold separately in a cut-down version for 3d.[6]

With his experience of journalism, government and academia, Beveridge made a formidable and effective propagandist. Through broadcasts, articles and half-leaks he made certain 'that the world knew it was coming'.[7] Indeed, as early as April 1942, a Home Intelligence report noted that 'Sir William Beveridge's proposals for an "all-in" social security scheme are said to be popular'.[8]

In the autumn, another report concluded: 'Three years ago, the term social security was almost unknown to the public as a whole. It now appears to be generally accepted as an urgent post-war need. It is commonly defined as 'a decent minimum standard of living for all'.[9]

In October, Brendan Bracken, the Minister of Information, wrote to Churchill saying: 'I have good reason to believe that some of Beveridge's friends are playing politics and that when the report appears there will be an immense amount of ballyhoo about the importance of implementing the recommendations without delay.'[10]

Bracken was right. Beveridge and his friends were playing

6   P. Addison, *The Road to 1945*, Jonathan Cape, London, 1975, p. 217.

7   Timmins, op. cit., p. 40.

8   Ibid., p. 41.

9   Addison, op. cit., pp. 215–16.

10   Ibid., p. 216.

politics and doing everything they could to grow the state. There is clear evidence that Beveridge understood the implications of his arguments and tactics. For example, in mid-November 1942, just a few weeks before the report's publication, he told the *Daily Telegraph* that his proposals would take Britain: '... half-way to Moscow'.[11]

Significantly, after the war, two papers marked 'secret' and providing a detailed commentary on Beveridge's plan were found in Hitler's bunker. One ordered that publicity should be avoided, but if mentioned the report should be used as: '... obvious proof that our enemies are taking over national-socialist ideas'.[12] The other report provided an official assessment of the plans and reported them as being no 'botch-up': '... a consistent system ... of remarkable simplicity ... superior to the current German social insurance in almost all points'.[13]

Although members of the Labour, Liberal and Communist parties were clearly in favour of Beveridge's plans – and in partic-ular the idea of a National Health Service – Churchill reacted on 21 March 1943. In a broadcast entitled 'After the War' he promised: '... national compulsory insurance for all classes for all purposes from the cradle to the grave'.[14] It was therefore Churchill, rather than Beveridge, who defined the plans in terms of running 'from the cradle to the grave' as he signed the wartime coalition up to its key recommendations and the idea of a National Health Service.

In February 1944 the Churchill-led government published White Papers on a National Health Service and Employment

11   Timmins, op. cit., p. 41.
12   Ibid., p. 25.
13   Fritz Grunder, *Beveridge Meets Bismarck*, York Papers, vol. 1, p. 69.
14   For more information see Addison, op. cit., p. 228.

Policy. It set up a Ministry of National Insurance and delivered the 1944 Education Act. A housing White Paper followed in March 1945, and on 11 June, as virtually the final act of the coalition government, the Family Allowances Act became law.

From the outset the health White Paper, *A National Health Service*, was seen as a bold and far reaching initiative. It asserted that everybody: '… irrespective of means, age, sex, or occupation shall have equal opportunity to benefit from the best and most up-to-date medical and allied services available'; that the service should be 'comprehensive' for all who wanted it; that it should be 'free of charge', and that it should promote good health 'rather than only the treatment of bad'.[15]

As such, it was now certain that a National Health Service, largely tax funded, free at the point of use and comprehensive, covering family doctors, dentists, hospitals and more besides, would become a reality.

As Minister of Health in the post-war Labour government, Aneurin Bevan was not only to capitalise on the intellectual and institutional tide of the age but to establish the NHS in the wake of a greatly expanded wartime state. In 1948, just prior to the appointed day of the NHS's commencement, the government issued a leaflet to every home in the country. It contained in black and white the promise that was supposed to encapsulate the new health service. It asserted that the NHS: '… will provide you with all medical, dental and nursing care. Everyone – rich or poor – can use it'.[16]

The key here was the word *all*. The state was going to offer

---

15   Michael Foot, *Aneurin Bevan, A Biography*, vol. 1: 1879–1945; vol. 2: 1945–60, Four Square, 1966, 1973; vol. 2, p. 131.

16   Department of Health leaflet announcing the NHS, July 1948.

comprehensive, universal and unlimited healthcare for everyone, whatever their need.

In early July 1948 the *Daily Mail* commented:

> On Monday morning you will wake up in a new Britain, in a state which 'takes over' its citizens six months before they are born, providing care and free services for their birth, for their early years, their schooling, sickness, workless days, widowhood and retirement. All this with free doctoring, dentistry and medicine – free bath-chairs, too, if needed – for 4/11d out of your weekly pay packet. You begin paying next Friday.[17]

The reality of rationing

Today, more than half a century on, it is arguable that the NHS has never made good its early promise. Beyond the simplistic world of media impression, rationing through a number of means has always been rife in the NHS and patients have often been denied the high-quality treatment and care by which they would best be served.

In reality, it did not take the 1945 Labour government long to realise that the NHS was not going to keep up with (or reduce, as some had suggested) people's demand for healthcare.[18] As Celia Hall, medical editor of the *Independent*, recalled in 1989:

> I remember a Medical Officer of Health in Birmingham, now dead, telling me they were so terrified that there would be a stampede for everything free on the day that the staff

---

17   *Daily Mail*, 3 July 1948.
18   Rudolf Klein, *The Politics of the National Health Service*, 2nd edn, Longman, London, 1989, p. 35.

> arrived early and literally barricaded themselves into their
> offices, peering out. Needless to say, this being Britain, soon
> after 9 o'clock a neat, orderly and not very long queue of
> mothers and babies formed up outside.[19]

While a number of experts had popularised the view that there might be an 'initial surge' in demand for spectacles and false teeth but that demand would then decrease, it soon became clear that such theorising was wrong. Within eighteen months of the service having been established, Bevan was himself admitting that there were problems. He commented: 'I shudder to think of the ceaseless cascade of medicine which is pouring down British throats at this time.'[20]

While he had been aware of the unpredictability of the costs of the service in advance, telling Hugh Dalton that it would take a full year's experience to understand them, he had also initially insisted that the NHS's high costs would decrease as the backlog of disease was treated.[21]

Back in 1944, Bevan's White Paper, *A National Health Service*, estimated that the service would cost taxpayers £132 million per year. This was revised upwards, however, to £152 million in 1946 and again to £230 million just before the Act came into force in July 1948. In its first full year of operation (1949–50) the NHS actually ended up costing £305 million, and it required a supplementary estimate of £98 million.[22]

---

19 Alice Law, recalling 5 July 1948, in Peter Hennessy, *Never Again, Britain 1945–51*, Jonathan Cape, London, 1992, p. 174.

20 C. Webster, *The Health Services since the War*, Association of Community Health Councils, London, 1996, p. 145.

21 Timmins, op. cit., p. 132.

22 Klein, op. cit., p. 34.

The inaccuracy of the estimates can be attributed to a number of factors. The first was that the early projections of cost assumed that demand would remain roughly constant, despite there being no price constraints on demand: the service being 'free' at the point of use.

Second, contemporary social and medical developments exacerbated the problems created by an absence of any price constraints on demand, not least because medical advances at the time meant that there was a dramatic expansion in the type and range of health services that could be made available:

> Streptomycin was not the only medical advance that became available. In the twenty-first century it is easily forgotten that the NHS has always had to absorb such costs to survive. In the service's first eighteen months other new antibiotics became available. So did tubocurarine, the muscle relaxant still in use today which rapidly widened the types of surgery which could be performed. Pernicious anaemia became treatable for the first time, new prophylactics became available for diphtheria, while cortisone, the first effective treatment for rheumatoid arthritis, was discovered. Many of these new treatments were both scarce and horrendously expensive. It was evidently impossible instantly to 'universalise the best'. It was, however, possible rationally to extend it by limiting the new treatments initially to specialist centres before falling prices allowed their more general use: the NHS's first – and perennial – answer to the rationing issue.[23]

Government realised early on that it could not afford a health service that was entirely free at the point of use. Although this

---

23 Timmins, op. cit., pp. 131–2.

was one of the founding principles of Bevan's NHS, it was actually abandoned within five years of the 1944 White Paper. In 1949, an amending Act was passed to allow the levying of a one-shilling charge on prescriptions.[24] By 1950 the system was under such pressure that one commentator, Cecil Palmer, went so far as to state in his seminal *The British Socialist Ill-Faire State*:

> Today, Great Britain is short of doctors and nurses. Our hospital services are being drastically economised, and building new ones to relieve the pressure of public demand is virtually suspended in consequence of largely inevitable cuts in our capital expenditure programmes. The much-publicised new clinics, which we were led to believe would solve most of the doctors' domestic and professional problems and incontestably make miserable patients happy, have not materialised and never will do so in a constipated socialist economy that is constantly under the necessity of robbing Peter to pay Paul.[25]

After the Conservative election victory of 1951, further charges were introduced for prescriptions, spectacles and dental treatment. Indeed, it was as far back as 1956 that the system of levying prescription charges by the number of items prescribed was first introduced.

The aim of these charging mechanisms was to simultaneously open a new source of funding revenue for the NHS while also deterring 'frivolous' demand for healthcare. But these measures proved to be grossly inadequate. For while there was some slowing in the rate of increase in the prescriptions issued, the revenue

---

24 Jim Bourlet, *Reality and the Future of UK Healthcare*, Independent Healthcare Association, London, 1994, p. 3.

25 Royal Commission on the National Health Service, Cmnd 7615, 1979, p. 436.

raised was never as significant as the Treasury would have liked. In 1950/51, charges contributed less than one per cent to the NHS budget, and even their largest contribution later in the decade was only 5.3 per cent.[26]

Another check to demand was a more deliberate rationing of supply through scarcity rather than through price. While doctors who worked in NHS hospitals had been encouraged at first to treat their patients according to need, and not to be deterred by financial considerations, the imposition of cash limits soon turned them into allocators of scarce resources.

More than minimal care was denied to cases where there was little chance of successful recovery, particularly to young children or the elderly with serious conditions. Indeed, healthcare for everyone else was provided sparingly by international standards. In the late 1970s, for example, coronary artery bypass operations were performed about ten times more frequently pro rata in the USA than in Britain; and where these did not increase life expectancy, they tended to reduce adverse symptoms such as pain. While US doctors responded to complaints about pain, British doctors have tended to pay more attention to the probable increases in life expectancy, or the improvements in a 'quality of life' not always synonymous with an absence of serious discomfort.[27]

The supply of healthcare has again been rationed still further by queuing. Crowded waiting rooms are common in most general practices and outpatient departments. And queues have become a fact of life for inpatients, often with long waiting periods for those operations given priority. Even in the 1980s and 1990s, after years

---

26 Klein, op. cit., p. 39.
27 Henry J Aron and William R. Schwartz, *The Painful Prescription: Rationing Hospital Care*, Brookings Institution, Wahsington, DC, 1984, p. 67.

of reforms designed to cut waiting lists, the median time to have a hernia repaired was more than ten weeks and the median was fourteen weeks for having a cataract treated.[28] The waiting times for many other less urgent procedures have usually been measured in months.

Certain health services have never been provided by the NHS, reducing the demand on its resources still further. Most forms of cosmetic surgery have rarely been available, and facelifts, liposuction, hair transplants and sex change operations have never been provided, except where they have been deemed necessary for reasons of health or as part of some other form of treatment. Other services have been provided on a minimal basis too. Much psychiatry, the treatment of infertility and substance misuse services remain cases in point.

Against the popular view that the NHS exists to provide 'free' and virtually unlimited healthcare, history demonstrates that the supply of NHS services has always been limited in significant ways. In reality, people have never had an absolute right to free and equal treatment on demand in the NHS. What they have had, in the main, is an unlimited right of access to a waiting list from which (with a few exceptions) they will not be excluded.

This right of access is not equivalent to a right to treatment, as any notional right to treatment has little value in practice if it is available only at the end of a two-year waiting time. The right to healthcare is unlimited in the long term, but is strictly limited in the short term when healthcare is actually required, at the very least, to relieve pain or discomfort.

---

28   Klein, op. cit., p. 155.

The reality of investment

As part of the 1946 Act's nationalisation process, NHS hospital building was to be financed by central government grants and funded out of general taxation and national insurance contributions. In the early years, however, the government made very little investment in its nationalised health estate. Not until the mid-1950s did a gradual release of funding allow new hospital building in some areas: and only then on a very limited basis.

Then, in July 1960, Enoch Powell became the Minister of Health. He arrived at a time of growing economic concern, which in government circles culminated in the 1961 Plowden Report.[29] It attempted to reconcile the Treasury's requirement for an annual budget in order to control spending with the demands of state welfare policy, including the NHS. The result was a five-year rolling programme which was approved each year by the Expenditure Survey Committee but was then subject to revision in each annual bid.

It was this work which started to address the fundamental issue of expenditure and the NHS's problems concerning capital investment. For during the first decade of the NHS, not a single new hospital had been built. None was even approved until 1956.[30] In the early 1960s the hospital estate that was in use was either that inherited from the independent sector or from local government. To address the problem Powell raised a number of NHS charges, including a doubling of the prescription charge from 1s to 2s (10p) an item.[31]

---

29 *Report on the Control of Public Expenditure* (the Plowden Report), Cmnd 1432, HMSO, London, 1961.

30 *A Hospital Plan for England and Wales*, Cmnd 1604, HMSO, London, 1962, pp. 1–2, 13.

31 Timmins, op. cit., p. 208.

The higher charges were in part to finance the great 'Hospital Plan', which was finally launched in January 1962. It aimed at a £500 million programme over a decade to build 90 new hospitals, drastically remodel 134 more and provide 356 further improvement schemes each costing more than £100,000.

While there had been a few hospital extensions, some new operating theatres, outpatient departments and minor refurbishments, in the thirteen years since 1948 only £157 million had been spent nationally: well under a third of the figure now proposed by Powell.

From the mid-1960s onwards, however, the consensus of the post-war settlement came under increasing pressure in a number of ways. With successive financial and economic crises, capital spending was cut. As such: 'By the mid-1970s, the wave of capital investment that had inaugurated the hospital plan for the NHS was effectively at an end.'[32]

In reality, even at the dawn of the 21st century much of the NHS estate that had been taken from the independent sector in the late 1940s '… still retains many pre-NHS features and a significant proportion of the stock predates the First World War'.[33]

This reality is significant because Beveridge originally believed that the NHS would raise the general level of health and fitness of the nation and increase national prosperity through a reduction of sickness absence to such a point that it would fundamentally raise people's productivity. As such, he believed the NHS would

---

32   D. Gaffney, A. M. Pollock, D. Price and J. Shaoul, 'NHS capital expenditure and the Private Finance Initiative – expenditure', *HM Treasury, Financial Statement and Budget Report 1999–2000*, HMSO, London, 1999.

33   Ibid.

broadly pay for itself or at the very least not be subject to endlessly rising costs.

In reality, the economic crises of the 1960s and 1970s led government to seek sources of capital funding other than government borrowing. And in 1973 regional health authorities were allowed for the first time to use the proceeds from land sales for reinvestment.[34] Mindful of Powell's original 1962 hospital plan, however, even by the 1990s: 'The plan ... [remained] ... unfulfilled, with only a third of the projected 224 schemes completed, and a third not yet started.'[35]

Since 1992, a high proportion of new capital investment in the NHS has been arranged under a scheme somewhat ironically known as the Private Finance Initiative (PFI) and more recently through Public Private Partnerships (PPP). Here the private sector can design, build, finance, own and even operate key areas of NHS provision, including some clinical services.[36] Although this policy was initially adopted by John Major's Conservative government, it was actively embraced by subsequent Labour administrations: 'In the absence of new capital, NHS trusts have no other recourse but to pursue the private finance initiative to finance new investment.'[37]

In recent years, under the general rubric of PPPs, the government has championed a whole raft of market-oriented NHS reforms. In 2000 the Secretary of State for Health, Alan Milburn, signed a Concordat with the representative body of Britain's by now re-emergent independent health and social care sector: the Independent

34 R. Meara, *Unfreezing the Assets: NHS estate management in the 1980s*, King's Fund Institute Research Report 11, Kings Fund, London, 1991.

35 Gaffney et al., op. cit.

36 For more see ibid.

37 Ibid.

Healthcare Association (IHA).[38] Under this agreement, the NHS could send its patients to independent hospitals and clinics for treatment and care.[39] Between 2000 and 2003 more than 250,000 NHS-funded patients received treatment and care in the independent sector and others were sent to private hospitals abroad.

In 2001, the government made it clear that it wanted the private sector to design, build and operate a new generation of Independent Sector Treatment Centres (ISTCs) for the benefit of NHS-funded patients. Soon after, the government named the private companies selected to bid for the contracts. All of them were foreign new market entrants, thereby underlining a new era of supply-side reform.[40]

Similarly, the government also made it clear that it wanted to establish a new generation of independent Foundation Hospitals. As such, the government wanted the best NHS hospitals to be 'set free' from Whitehall control and to have a greater say over how they developed and from where they raised their capital.[41]

Overall, the historical direction of travel in the NHS is clear: selling off NHS land, the PFI, PPPs, the Concordat with the IHA, ISTCs and Foundation Trusts all point to an increasingly market-oriented future. Slowly, the NHS is being redefined as a funder of healthcare but not as a provider or owner of the facilities in which the services are delivered.

---

38 The Independent Healthcare Association was the main representative body of the UK's independent health and social care sector. After more than fifty years of work it closed in 2004.

39 For a detailed overview of the Concordat and how it came about, see A. M. Pollock, *NHS plc: The Privatisation of Our Healthcare*, Verso, London, 2004, pp. 66–8.

40 Ibid., pp. 68–71.

41 Ibid., pp. 71–7.

The reality of class

Theoretically the NHS exists to treat people of all social classes in an equitable manner according to need. In practice, however, this has never actually happened.

Using the Registrar General's classification, the life expectancy of a child with parents in social class V (unskilled manual) is more than seven years fewer than that for a child whose parents are in social class I (professional). Male manual workers have premature death rates 45 per cent higher than non-manual workers.[42] The number of premature deaths connected with manual work is greater than the total number of deaths from strokes, infectious diseases, accidents, lung cancer and other respiratory diseases combined.[43]

Significantly, the socio-economic differences in mortality are not simply confined to a few isolated diseases associated with particular occupations or lifestyles. Of the 66 'major list' causes of death among men, according to Adonis and Pollard 62 are more common in social groups IV and V than among all other social groups.[44]

Equally important in all of this is the persistence of inequalities in access to healthcare. Analyses of GP consultations have repeatedly shown that higher-social-class patients invariably receive more sophisticated explanations and details of their treatment than lower-social-class patients,[45] and that the middle classes spend more time on average with their GP than those

---

42 Andrew Adonis and Stephen Pollard, *A Class Act: The Myth of Britain's Classless Society*, Hamish Hamilton, London, 1998, p. 171.

43 Ibid.

44 Ibid., p. 172.

45 Ibid.

with working-class backgrounds.[46] Famously, Julian Le Grand has shown that, relative to need, professional and managerial groups receive more than 40 per cent more NHS spending per illness episode than those people in semi-skilled and unskilled jobs.

Commenting on the NHS's legitimacy, Adonis and Pollard concluded in their 1998 book, *A Class Act: The Myth of Britain's Classless Society*:

> ... in reality the NHS owes its effectiveness and popularity in large part to the fact that it is not egalitarian. The comfortably off revere the NHS in no small part because they get a good bargain out of it, and are thus happy to feel good about themselves by continuing to pay for what they are told is a subsidy to the poor.[47]

The reality of employment

Sixty years on from its inception and the NHS actually mirrors the class rigidities it was supposed to undermine. As the largest employer in Europe, and the most important pillar of Britain's welfare state, the service employs more than one million people or more than 3.5 per cent of the country's total workforce[48] – it is a 'microcosm of class structure':

> At the top of the NHS are the hospital-based consultants (at the very top are the consultants of the London teaching hospitals) ... Below the consultants is the upper middle class of the medical profession – the senior managers, who may earn as much as the consultants but who are the

---

46 Michael Benzeval, Ken Judge and Margaret Whitehead, *Tackling Inequalities in Health*, Kings Fund, London, 1995, p. 104.

47 Pollard and Adonis, op. cit., p. 180.

48 Ibid., p. 155.

nouveaux riches of the service. Next comes the middle middle class, the GPs – some through choice, some because they have not quite made it. An increasing number of these are female – often because women realise pretty soon that they are unlikely to make it up the hospital career ladder. There is then a dramatic drop to the skilled, lower middle class: the nurses, therapists, technologists and technicians, who are mainly female. And below them is the proletariat – the auxiliary, ancillary and service personnel, who are overwhelmingly female.[49]

Today, the NHS has more women employees than any comparable organisation. Women represent more than 75 per cent of non-medical staff and 45 per cent of general managers. Yet they account for only 28 per cent of chief executives and senior managers and around 20 per cent of consultants. Also there are very few black or ethnic minority senior managers.

If one looks at the NHS from the inside and how it is staffed and organised the reality is clear: '… if we look at how it is structured, and at those who work in it – we can see that it is indeed a fair microcosm of Britain's class structure. Just as the classless society is itself a myth, so too is the comforting classless NHS'.[50]

The reality of care

Today, the NHS has many hundreds of thousands of people on waiting lists and countless tens of thousands trying to get on to them. After years of reform and several extra tens of billions of pounds thrown at the service, of 4 million patients admitted

49   Ibid., pp. 155–6.
50   Ibid., p. 169.

to NHS hospitals for routine treatment in 2007, more than half still waited more than eighteen weeks. While government ministers frequently shy away from talking about the parlous realities of waiting times, figures indicate that 12 per cent – almost half a million people – waited more than a year for their treatment and care in 2006/07.[51]

A Department of Health analysis of 208,000 people admitted to hospital in March 2007 indicated that 48 per cent were taken into operating theatres within eighteen weeks of a GP sending them for hospital diagnosis. Some 30 per cent, however, waited more than thirty weeks.

Today, in many NHS hospitals, more than 10 per cent of patients pick up infections and illnesses they did not have prior to being admitted.[52] And according to the Malnutrition Advisory Group up to 60 per cent of NHS hospital patients can be undernourished during inpatient stays.[53]

In many areas, it is increasingly difficult for people to get a timely appointment with an NHS GP or even to find an NHS dentist.[54]

The political economy of government failure

Sixty years on from the inception of the NHS it is possible to judge

51 David Rose, 'One in eight patients still waiting more than a year but "targets will be met"', *The Times*, 8 June 2007.

52 Department of Public Health and Policy, London School of Hygiene and Tropical Medicine, *Research Briefing: Hospital Acquired Infections*, no. 5, London, 2001.

53 See www.nhs.uk/nhsmagazine/archive/apr/features/this16.htm. The MAG's report was released on 11 November 2003.

54 Alison Hardie and Ian Johnston, 'Vicious circle of blame over dental crisis', *The Scotsman*, 1 February 2005. See also Adonis and Pollard, op. cit., p. 179.

the service by its deeds. One can scrutinise its rationing, its low levels of capital investment, and its inequitable and inadequate results. One can profile its internal structure by class, race and gender, and one can analyse the ways in which its political masters are increasingly endeavouring to 'crisis manage' by allowing the gradual rediscovery of various forms of independent healthcare.

As politicians of all parties arguably turn full circle and look to the independent sector for solutions in provision, one also quickly encounters the rediscovery of non-state self-help in important areas of healthcare funding.

As people become less tolerant of poor service, and less willing to act as passive recipients 'grateful for what they receive', what is now true in so many other areas of life is rapidly becoming apparent in healthcare. In many ways, people's attitudes to healthcare have already changed. In a less deferential age in which ever larger numbers of people have a university education, and consumer information flows freely on the Internet, people are more aware of their choices and their powers of exit.

Back in 2003, Labour politicians publicly claimed that it was only the Conservatives who wanted to encourage various forms of private health funding. Yet under Labour's governance, more than 6.5 million people have private medical insurance and another 6 million people are covered by private health cash plans. Millions more choose from a wide range of other options, such as acute care self-funding and paying privately for a range of alternative therapies. In contrast to the original promise that the NHS 'would provide all medical, dental and nursing care'[55]: 'In dentistry, more than a third of the population has now abandoned the NHS and

---

55   This quote is from a leaflet describing the role of the NHS delivered to every British home in July 1948. It was produced by the Ministry of Health.

relies solely on independent sector treatment. And more than eight million people pay privately for a range of complementary medical therapies every year'.[56]

According to research published in the *Daily Telegraph*[57] more than 3.5 million trade unionists – more than 50 per cent of the Trade Union Congress's 6.8 million members – enjoy the benefits of private health cash and medical insurance schemes. At a time when the country's political class is trying to get itself off the hook of past promises by exploiting the rhetoric of public–private partnerships, many independent sector organisations already have formal agreements with trade unions or have large numbers of trade unionists in their memberships. Some schemes offer private medical, permanent health or critical illness cover. Others offer private health cash plans that pay for services that include items such as dentistry, ophthalmics, physiotherapy, chiropody, podiatry, maternity services, allergy testing, hospital inpatient stays, nursing home stays, hospital day case admissions, convalescence, home help, mental health and psychiatric treatment, and even the use of an ambulance.

Today, independent sector healthcare schemes abound and many are in the not-for-profit tradition. A cursory survey is provided in the annexe to this chapter. As is clear from the annexe, many so-called public sector trade unions such as Unison have formal links with private medical cash plan schemes such as Medicash:

> Today, independent sector not-for-profit organisations such
> as the Benenden Hospital, Bristol Contributory Welfare

---

56   Independent Healthcare Association data, May 2002.
57   Daniel Kruger, 'Why half trade union members have private health', *Daily Telegraph*, 11 September 2001.

Association, BUPA, Civil Service Healthcare Society,
Hospitals Savings Association ... Wakefield Health Scheme,
Westfield Health and many other similar bodies, have
millions of trade unionists in their combined memberships.

Many public sector trade unions such as Unison even
have formal links with private health cash schemes such as
Medicash and promote them on their internet sites. These
schemes are an important and growing source of revenue
for the independent sector and add to the diversity of the
overall health market.[58]

In an article he wrote before he died in 1994, but which was
not published in the *Daily Telegraph* until 1996, Sir Keith Joseph
argued that market-based institutions in civil society should be
rediscovered and applied to health and welfare. Prophetically, he
wrote:

> My own favourite strategy to give every home a stake in the
> economy is to allow Friendly Societies to recover much of
> the role they relinquished over this century. No pension
> fund, state or corporate, conveys a sense of ownership or
> participation. I believe the small mutual status of Friendly
> Societies helps the quality of co-operative intimacy.[59]

Six years on from this statement, the Labour Secretary of State
for Health Alan Milburn stated:

> Last month, I met with the chief executives of the three star
> [NHS] Trusts. They had a list of further specific restrictions
> that they wanted to have removed from them and we are
> now considering how best to do so. But they also asked us
> to go further. If they were as good as we agreed they were,

---

58   Edward Vaizey (ed.), *The Blue Book on Health: Radical Thinking on the Future of the NHS*, Politico's, London, 2002, p. 99.

59   Sir Keith Joseph, 'Why the Tories are the real party of the stakeholder', *Daily Telegraph*, 12 January 1996.

why could they not become independent not-for-profit institutions with just an annual cash for performance contract and no further form of performance management from the centre?[60]

In outlining the government's ideas for genuinely independent 'Foundation Hospitals', Milburn continued:

The middle ground between state-run public and shareholder-led private structures is where there has been growing interest in recent years. Both the Right – through organisations like the Institute of Directors – and the Left – through the Co-operative Movement – have been examining the case for new forms of organisation such as mutuals or public interest companies … [61]

Keith Joseph had warned of such politics emanating from New Labour back in 1996. He well understood that the race was on to capture such terrain between the two major parties. He wrote in his *Daily Telegraph* article: 'I wonder if the Labour Party, hungry for radical ideas, might steal such notions and apply them first. I regard Frank Field MP as our most dangerous opponent as he treats liberal market ideas as serious options, and not merely as misanthropy.'[62]

Capturing traditionally Conservative and classical liberal terrain in one fell swoop, Milburn concluded:

In many other European countries there are many not-for-profit voluntary or charity-run hospitals all providing care

---

60 Secretary of State for Health, Rt Hon. Alan Milburn, MP, speech to New Health Network, 15 January 2002.

61 Ibid.

62 Joseph, op. cit.

to the public health care system. There are private sector organisations doing the same. Similar steps are already starting here. We are in negotiation with BUPA ... [63]

The idea of the NHS repositioning itself as the regulatory overseer of a market of private providers over the next decade or so is plausible. It is also possible that the NHS might over time mutate to become the health funder of last resort.

Nevertheless, in 2008 it remains doubtful that such a world would amount to a genuine market in healthcare. What would be more likely to emerge would be a rediscovery of the complex medical corporatism of previous centuries – a world of private health provision and funding that is again predicated on a set of professional monopoly powers gained through legislative favour. As in earlier eras of medical history, what seems most likely is a quasi-market driven by the political economy of regulation, not a real market based on the principles of consumer sovereignty and producer reputation.

For all the manifest failings of the NHS and the growing acceptance of a limited range of private solutions, there is still little in public discourse to fundamentally challenge the statist notions that underpin professional monopoly power in health. Few commentators challenge such illusory notions of independence or go on to question the fundamental nature and impact of statutory regulation and monopoly power.

One of the few to do so is Professor David Gladstone.[64] For him the General Medical Council (GMC) is far from being an

63 Milburn, op. cit.
64 Dr David Gladstone, *Opening Up the Medical Monopoly*, Adam Smith Institute, London, 1992.

independent regulator. He argues that, maintaining its monopoly power in statute, throughout its history it has shunned consumer control and always sought domination from within the profession as well as the wider establishment. Gladstone spelled out the adverse impact of such arrangements in an article he wrote and published in *The Times*: '… longer than necessary training, intolerable conditions for those beneath the consultant level, a system of patronage and personal recommendation for appointments, limits on the number of consultancy appointments'.[65]

The idea that doctors should be accountable to their patients seems at face value to be clear. The GMC was formed, however, to ensure not only that the ethical standards of the profession were maintained but also that doctors should remain accountable to the state. In other words, through the Medical Act of 1858 it was: '… the state [which] ratified medicine's claims to be an autonomous self-governing ethical profession'.[66]

In reality, the Act was the product of a highly charged and protracted political and parliamentary debate. Yet once agreed, it ultimately '… charged the Council to regulate the medical profession on behalf of the state, to oversee medical education and to maintain a register of qualified medical practitioners'.[67]

In open markets, the threat of entry by newcomers not only puts pressure on prices but also encourages innovation and the discovery of optimal outcomes. In monopolies, however, resistance to innovation is strong. Unchallenged professional conservatism and a resistance to change become the dominant ethos.

---

65 David Gladstone, 'The doctor's dilemma', *The Times*, 2 March 1992.

66 Roy Porter, *Disease, Medicine and Society in England 1550–1860*, Macmillan, London, 1987, p. 52.

67 Margaret Stacey, *Regulating British Medicine*, John Wiley, London, 1992, p. 85.

In 2008, it is ironic that, after more than half a century of the NHS, and several hundred years of politicians bestowing monopoly powers on medical professionals (initially through the Royal Colleges), it is governmental failure in health systems which can be argued to cause precisely those problems most popularly associated with notions of 'market failure'.

For after many decades of politicised healthcare the resultant and statist problems of monopoly, consumer ignorance, neglect of the poor and sick, lack of provision and moral hazard are clear for all to see.

Annexe: independent healthcare schemes

The Benenden Hospital – www.thesociety.co.uk – friendly society scheme serves 1 million British Telecom, Post Office and civil service workers and their families. Established in 1905, the Benenden is one of the largest independent hospitals in the country. It works in partnership with a national network of other not-for-profit independent hospitals and has a close relationship with many tens of thousands of trade unionists.

BUPA – www.bupa.com – is a mutual offering a wide range of private medical insurance and health cash benefits. Established in 1947, the British United Provident Association is the amalgamation of seventeen historic provident associations and today covers more than three million people: many of whom are trade union members.[68]

---

68   BUPA estimate that some 10 per cent of their members are in trades unions and professional associations.

The Birmingham Hospital Saturday Fund – www.bhsf.co.uk – is a mutual that specialises in private health cash benefits. It has 150,000 workers in membership, a high proportion of whom are trade unionists.

The Civil Service Healthcare Society – www.cshealthcare.co.uk – was founded in the 1920s. It has more than 25,000 people in membership. A mutual offering private medical insurance, its members are primarily workers in the public sector.

The Communication Workers Friendly Society – www.cwfs.co.uk – is a mutual offering private sickness benefits. Having a special relationship with union members in the postal and telecommunications industries, it is strongly aligned with the Communications Workers Union.[69]

The Dentists' Provident Society – www.dentistsprovident.co.uk – is a mutual offering permanent health insurance, private health cash benefits and accident and sickness benefits. Most members are dental surgeons, many of whom work in the NHS.

Exeter Friendly Society – www.exeterfriendly.co.uk – offers private medical insurance and is one of the best-known healthcare friendly societies working in Britain.

Health Shield – www.healthshield.co.uk – is a friendly society with more than 120 years of experience. It offers a range of private health cash benefits.

---

69 The Communications Workers Friendly Society is open about this relationship on its website: www.cwfs.co.uk.

Health Sure – www.healthsure.org.uk – is a mutual offering private health cash benefits. Over the years, many members of the Unison trade union have been in membership.

Holloway Friendly Society – www.holloway.co.uk – specialises in permanent health insurance and sickness benefits. Historically, it has a close relationship with trade unionists in customs and excise.

HSA Simply Health – www.hsa.co.uk – is a mutual organisation that offers private medical insurance and cash benefits to more than three million people, many of whom are members of trade unions.[70]

The Independent Order of Odd Fellows Manchester Unity – www.oddfellows.co.uk – is a friendly society that offers sickness benefits and medical cash benefits.

Medicash – www.medicash.org – is a mutual organisation that offers private health cash benefits and has many trade unionists as members. It works particularly closely with the police and fire services and has a formal partnership with Unison at *www.medicash.org/unison/*. It traditionally makes charitable donations to the NHS and has more than 200,000 workers in membership.

Nuffield Hospitals – www.nuffieldhospitals.org.uk – is a charitable organisation that offers a national network of more than forty not-for-profit hospitals. Nuffield has close links with a wide

---

70   HSA estimate that some 30 per cent of their cash plan members are in trade unions.

range of worker groups and actively welcomes trade unionists into membership.

Shepherds Friendly Society – www.shepherds.co.uk – is a friendly society offering sickness benefits and permanent health insurance. It welcomes trade unionists into membership.

Wakefield Health Scheme – www.wdhcs.com – offers private health cash benefits and has more than fifty thousand workers in membership. Many of them are current or former trade unionists.

Western Provident Association – www.wpa.org.uk – is a mutual organisation that offers a wide range of private medical insurance and health cash benefits.

Westfield Health – www.westfieldhealth.com – offers private health cash benefits. It has many trade unionists in membership and historically has a particularly close relationship with members of the Transport and General Workers Union. It has more than 350,000 workers in membership and traditionally has an exhibition stand at the annual Labour Party conference.

3 THE IDEA OF MARKET FAILURE IN MODERN HEALTH ECONOMICS

Today, neoclassical criticisms of genuine free markets in healthcare abound and too many so-called free marketeers fall into the trap of defending private sector arrangements that are invariably underpinned by nationalised labour markets. As such, this chapter examines notions of market failure in mainstream health economics and examines the dominant political and economic paradigm of our age.

Market failure, public goods and health economics

By the end of the nineteenth century and for the first half of the twentieth century, the command economy model was ascendant. Whether further encouraged in Britain by the translation of Karl Marx's work into English in the early 1890s, or by the rise of an essentially middle-class Fabian elite that actively embraced incremental socialism,[1] the early twentieth century saw a rise in the ideas that popularised state planning, public sector benevolence and notions of equity.

Even in the middle of the twentieth century, when the socially democratic economics of Keynes was suggesting that politicians should run society through the principles of 'management by an

---

1   Hal Draper, 'The two souls of socialism', *New Politics*, 5(1), Winter 1966.

intelligent elite', many Conservatives found it attractive to argue for a so-called 'ordered middle way' between orthodox socialism and laissez-faire liberalism.[2] It was in this world of pre-Popperian thought that Harold Macmillan wrote: 'The next step forward, therefore, in our social thinking is to move on from "piece-meal planning" to national planning – from the consideration of each industry or service separately to a consideration of them all collectively.'[3]

Given that Conservatism rested during this period upon such holistic notions as the subsumation of the individual to the politics of community, nation and empire, it is perhaps understandable that in the 1930s many leading Conservatives accepted the fashionable argument for greater social planning and more state intervention. Now convinced by the arguments concerning market failure, Macmillan, for instance, asserted:

> Expert criticism has revealed the deficiencies of partial or piecemeal planning, and has made it clear that we must carry the idea of planning further, and evolve such a national scheme. We must take account of all the problems, and of all the repercussions of partial schemes with limited objectives. If we do not widen its scope, the whole idea of planning will be discredited.

---

2 It is curious how the existence of an alliance of statist Toryism and socialism has fallen out of any popular consciousness. One of the few studies that can be found is in B. Semmel, *Imperialism and State Reform: English Social-Imperial Thought, 1895–1914*, Harvard University Press, Cambridge, MA, 1960. There is a growing literature on eugenics, 'right wing' (that is, anti-capitalist and anti-liberal) social Darwinism and paternalism. See G. R. Searle, *The Quest for National Efficiency*, Oxford University Press, Oxford, 1971, and *Social Hygiene in Twentieth Century Britain*, Croom Helm, London, 1986; R. A. Soloway, *Demography and Degeneration: Eugenics and the Declining Birthrate in Twentieth Century Britain*, University of North Carolina Press, Chapel Hill, 1990.

3 H. Macmillan, *The Middle Way*, Macmillan, London, 1938, p. 176.

> ... The weakness of partial planning seems to me to
> arise from the incomplete and limited application of the
> principles of planning. The lesson of these errors, which I
> regard as errors of limitation, is not that we should retreat.
> On the contrary, we must advance, more rapidly and still
> further, upon the road of conscious regulation.[4]

In mid and late twentieth century Britain such notions provided the consensual backbone of mainstream political opinion. And where markets were not perceived as achieving socially desirable outcomes, economists invoked the now popular notions of market failure to suggest specific policies to 'correct' this.

Indeed, health economics – particularly as it emerged in Britain in the 1950s and beyond – has consistently emphasised the unique nature of healthcare, drawing on the view that market failure is somehow inherent and unavoidable. The conclusion reached is that, in this particular area of welfare, unfettered markets are wholly and inevitably inappropriate.

This view of market failure is common to those who have a general belief in free markets as well as those of a more collectivist disposition. To social democratic and collectivist writers on health and welfare such as Tawney, Titmuss and Laksi,[5] social justice and

---

4   Ibid., pp. 10–11.

5   R. H. Tawney, *The Agrarian Problem in the Sixteenth Century*, Longman, Green, London, 1912, *The Acquisitive Society*, Fontana, London, 1961 [1921], *Religion and the Rise of Capitalism*, Pelican, West Drayton, 1938 [1926], *Equality*, Unwin Books, London, 1964 [1931], 'Christianity and the social revolution', *New Statesman and Nation*, November 1935, *The Attack and Other Papers*, George Allen and Unwin, London, 1953, *The Radical Tradition. Twelve essays on politics, education and literature* (ed. Rita Hinden), Penguin, Harmondsworth, 1966; Richard Titmuss, 'The irresponsible society', Fabian Tract 232, April 1960, *Income, Distribution and Change*, London, 1962, *The Gift Relationship*, London, 1971, *Social Policy: An Intro-*

equality are the key activating themes. They regard resources as being available for collective use and consequently favour government intervention. They criticise the pursuance of personal advantage rather than the general good, believing that the former does not bring about the latter. The market is criticised for being undemocratic, insofar as these thinkers believe it encourages decisions to be taken by a small power elite, and other people are left to suffer at the hands of arbitrary distributional forces. The market is also said to be unjust because it distributes rewards that are unrelated to individual need or merit, and because the costs of economic change are also distributed arbitrarily.

Under the influence of the social democratic paradigm and its value judgements, a set of standard assumptions has come to inform most modern health economics from which a critique of the free market is derived. For example, in the standard textbook *The Economics of the Welfare State*,[6] the author, Nicholas Barr, asserts: 'Private markets allocate efficiently only if the standard assumptions hold – that is, perfect information, perfect competition, and no market failures such as external effects. The underlying question is why health care is "different" from equally vital commodities like food.'[7]

Barr immediately goes on to accept the modern – highly regulated and corporatist – health market as being in some way analogous to a real free market process. He writes: 'Does medical care conform with standard assumptions? First, are individuals perfectly

duction, London, 1974; Harold Laski, *Democracy in Crisis*, University of North Carolina Press, Chapel Hill, 1933, *Faith, Reason, and Civilisation*, Viking Press, London, 1944, *Liberty in the Modern State*, Allen & Unwin, London, 1948.

6   Nicholas Barr, *The Economics of the Welfare State*, 3rd edn, Oxford University Press, Oxford, 1988.

7   Ibid., p. 282.

informed about the nature of the product (in analytical terms, is their indifference map well defined)? The answer, clearly, is no.'[8]

Equating contemporary healthcare practices with a real market, he continues:

> In addition, individuals are often ignorant about which
> types of treatment are available, and about the outcome
> of different treatments, which is often problematic.
> Furthermore, what little the patient knows is generally
> learnt from the provider of medical services; and many types
> of treatment (e.g. setting a broken leg) are not repeated so
> that much of what a patient learns is of little future use.[9]

Barr is typical of many academic commentators. On matters of consumer choice and information, he simply operates within the given – statist – institutional boundaries, though ones set by the neoclassical economic framework, and therefore confidently asserts that with medical care:

- Much (though not all) the information is technically complex, so that a person would not necessarily understand the information even were it available.
- Mistaken choice is costlier and less reversible than with most other commodities.
- An individual generally does not have time to shop around if his condition is acute (contrast the situation with a car repair, which can be left until the car owner has enough information and can afford the repair).
- Consumers frequently lack the information to weigh one doctor's advice against another's.

8   Ibid.
9   Ibid.

- Health and healthcare have strongly emotive connotations – for example, ignorance may in part be a consequence of fear, superstition, etc.[10]

Barr acknowledges that in some areas, such as hi-fis and used cars, consumers can buy information from consumer magazines or have it provided by trade associations, but interestingly he forgets to mention advertising. Without justifying his argument, he goes on to state – as if an a priori truth – that:

> … health care is inherently a technical subject, so that there is a limit to what consumers could understand without themselves becoming doctors. The problem is exacerbated by the existence of groups who would not be able to make use of information even if they had it, such as victims of road accidents.[11]

There is no questioning here of whether healthcare really is more technically difficult or more challenging for consumers to understand than any of the other products mentioned – namely, motor cars and hi-fi systems.[12] There is no reference to the liberal argument that in a market consumers do not have to have perfect information or anything approaching it. Instead, they should have access to the commercial free speech, advertising and reputations that, over time, emerge from brands.

When it comes to health economics as a discipline there is usually little if any reference to the role of brands or market-driven reputation. Instead, there appears to be an implicit respect for the given boundaries of government intervention

---

10 Ibid., p. 283.
11 Ibid.
12 Ibid.

and statutory regulation. For instance, turning to prices, Barr continues:

> Here, again, it can be argued that most consumers are ignorant of what a particular form of treatment 'should' cost; and, because a great deal of medical care is not repeated, information often has no future use. Nor would it help if consumers were well informed about prices. Rational choice requires simultaneous knowledge both of prices and of the nature of the product (i.e. of both budget constraint and indifference map); knowledge of prices without adequate information about different types of treatment will not ensure efficiency.[13]

Tellingly, Barr immediately goes on to assert that:

> ... if the only problem were inadequate information about prices, the appropriate intervention would be regulation, either in the form of a published price list or through price controls. But where information about the nature of the product is imperfect, ignorance about prices adds further weight to the argument for more substantial state involvement.[14]

The whole debate is couched in favour of state interventionism and state control. From the straw man of so-called 'perfect information', the artificial edifice of imperfect prices is quickly established, without ever discussing whether the state can, in principle or in practice, correct the outcomes of so-called imperfect markets.

Again, working within given boundaries, health economists are quick to assert that: '... the market solution is insurance'.[15]

13 Ibid., p. 284.
14 Ibid.
15 Ibid., p. 285

And that: 'The real issue, therefore, is whether the private market can supply medical insurance efficiently.'[16]

Locked again into a world of similar a priori assumptions, health economists popularly assert that, when considering health insurance markets, there are five technical conditions that must hold:

> … the probability of needing treatment … must be independent across individuals, and less than one; it must be known or estimable; and there must be no substantial problem of adverse selection or moral hazard (the last three conditions adding up to perfect information on the part of the insurance company).[17]

Not only are current models of insurance viewed as being indicative of a real free market in healthcare – a notion which is itself highly questionable – but issues such as adverse selection and moral hazard are typically discussed only in terms of market failure, not state sector (or political) failure.

The idea that, in a democracy, state health and welfare systems normally adversely favour – and thereby disproportionately benefit – articulate middle-class recipients over poorer clients is usually excluded from textbooks. Similarly, the argument that state health and welfare systems can themselves encourage problems of moral hazard is normally marginalised or excluded from most mainstream literature. When these things are occasionally referred to, interventionist – not market-based – ideas are then usually invoked as the logical next step. Hence, the following statement concerning market failures in healthcare:

---

16   Ibid.
17   Ibid., p. 286.

Thus the lower-income individuals may have less information relevant to choices about health; in addition, they may be less able to make use of any information they acquire. In such cases intervention in the following forms may improve equity as well as efficiency.

Regulation would be concerned with the professional qualification of doctors and nurses, with drugs, and with medical facilities in both public and private sectors.

Where imperfect information causes under-consumption, a subsidy might be applied either to prices (e.g. free medical prescriptions) or to incomes.

… Where problems of inadequate information and inequality of power are serious, efficiency and equity may jointly be maximised by public allocation and/or production. In broad terms this depends on two factors: whether the private or public sectors is more efficient at producing health care; and whether monitoring of standards is more effective in one sector or the other.[18]

What starts out purporting to be about economics and an analysis of healthcare soon degenerates into what are effectively subjective and highly politicised assumptions concerning the constructed notion of market failure and the idea of state-supported equity. They can be regarded as subjective because Barr does not apply the same rigour of analysis in questioning the imperfections of state provision and intervention as he applies to the analysis of market failure.

Criticising much mainstream economics, Professor John Burton has argued in his paper 'Economics: still dismal after all these years'[19] that the bias against genuine market processes

18   Ibid., p. 290.
19   John Burton, 'Economics: still dismal after all these years', *Economic Notes*, 17,

generally occurs because students of economics are invariably taught to look at economic questions as a set of relatively simple and mathematically tractable equations. For him, the implicit assumption is that economic systems are one with a low order of complexity and therefore tractable using a mathematical system. He complains that:

> Repeated exposure to this assumption in a variety of guises (the Keynes and monetarist macro models, Marshallian and Walrasian models of markets, etc.), has the unfortunate consequence of ingraining a habit of thought in the student. He starts to believe that real world economic processes are non-complex systems, and that they are just as manipulable as the equation systems that he is taught to handle mathematically.[20]

Notions of market failure in today's NHS debate

While John Maynard Keynes argued that politicians essentially follow in the wake of economists and philosophers,[21] it is interesting to consider a keynote speech that Gordon Brown gave to the Social Market Foundation in February 2003.[22] Then Chancellor of the Exchequer, he argued that while the government should increasingly embrace the free market to build a strong economy and a fairer society, healthcare had to remain publicly

---

Libertarian Alliance, London, 1989.

20 Ibid.

21 John Maynard Keynes famously wrote: 'The ideas of economists and political philosophers ... are more powerful than is commonly understood. Indeed, the world is ruled by little else. Madmen in authority, who hear voices in the air, are distilling their frenzy from some academic scribbler of a few years back.'

22 3 February 2003.

funded and publicly provided. Breaking with traditional Labour thinking and initially embracing the benefits of a dynamic market economy, he began:

> Instead of being suspicious of competition, we should embrace it, recognising that without it vested interests accumulate ... Instead of being lukewarm about free trade, free trade not protectionism is essential to opportunity and security for all and instead of the old protectionism we advocate open markets. Instead of being suspicious of enterprise and entrepreneurs, we should celebrate the entrepreneurial culture ... Instead of extending regulation unnecessarily to restrict the scope of markets, we should systematically pinpoint services where regulation does not serve the public interest.[23]

It was not long, however, before Brown made it clear that there was a limit to his enthusiasm for free markets. He declared that healthcare should not be treated as a 'commodity bought and sold like any other'.[24] Arguing that 'essential public services' such as the NHS must remain under the purview of the state, he warned that if the market were ever allowed to intervene Labour would be: '... unable to deliver a Britain of opportunity and security for all'.[25]

Indeed, it was the passion of his resistance to free market reforms in the NHS which stood out from this important speech. Crucially, he argued that the government's promotion of markets must be combined with a 'clear and robust' recognition of their limits. And

---

23 'Brown goes for the free market (but not in the NHS)', *Daily Mail*, 4 February 2003, p. 2.
24 Ibid.
25 Ibid.

he highlighted the provision of healthcare as being a primary sector where market forces should not be allowed to operate:

> In healthcare we know that the consumer is not sovereign: use of healthcare is unpredictable and can never be planned by the consumer in the way that, for example, weekly food consumption can. With the consumer unable, as in a conventional market, to seek out the best product at the lowest price, the results of a market failure for the patient can be long term and catastrophic and irreversible.[26]

This speech highlights very clearly the dominance of the market failure paradigm as a fundamental notion deeply embedded in the contemporary healthcare debate. It exposed the presumptions and biases of major swathes of the political and intellectual class as well as a misunderstanding of the fundamental nature of the market process. For the story of the development of notions of market failure in healthcare can be viewed as the establishment of highly restrictive, artificial and ultimately counter-productive boundaries on discourse and debate. When it comes to the history of British healthcare and the NHS, expanded and popular notions of market failure have come to dominate popular mindset and opinion. Although there is now some evidence to suggest that ideas of 'government failure' are on the ascendant – and might themselves come to triumph in the future healthcare debate – there is clearly a very long way to go. We now move on to look in detail at the view of elite opinion concerning healthcare in Britain.

---

26   Ibid.

4 THE NHS AND PUBLIC AND ELITE OPINION

Public health and public opinion

In the central part of this monograph, we will examine what elite opinion – what some have described as the New Class, as discussed below – thinks about the NHS and alternative forms of health provision. Before this, we examine a comprehensive public opinion survey of the NHS and alternatives of private provision and financing.

Aneurin Bevan's declared aim, when he established the NHS, was to 'universalise the best'. As Nick Bosanquet and Stephen Pollard have suggested, however:

> … rather than universalising the best, its proudest boast should be that it has universalised the adequate. To ensure that everyone receives the best conceivable treatment has always been beyond even the generous financing the service has received … The story of the NHS so far … has instead been one of rationing scarce resources.[1]

And, given this reality of experience, Bosanquet and Pollard commissioned a survey of public opinion by MORI as Labour came to power in 1997.[2] The survey sought to explore in detail not

---

1   N. Bosanquet and S. Pollard, *Ready for Treatment: Popular Expectations and the Future of Health Care*, Social Market Foundation, London, 1997, p. 1.

2   Ibid., p. 39.

just what people wanted from the NHS over the next ten years, but what they expected.

Using a series of half-hour, one-to-one interviews, the research produced represented the most extensive survey undertaken into the attitudes of the British public on the NHS. A total of 2,012 interviews were conducted face-to-face, in-house, among adults aged fifteen and over. The research was carried out between 12 July and 3 August 1997 across Britain. Quotas were set for sex, age and working status and the data that resulted were weighted to the known population profile.

Almost two-thirds (64 per cent) of respondents said that they believed that people often make unnecessary visits to their GP because the service costs nothing at the point of use. Moreover:

> One in five (19 per cent) believe strongly that this is the case and one-quarter disagree (although only 6 per cent disagree strongly). [Social classes] DEs are more inclined than ABs to think that people make unnecessary visits.
>
> Fewer, albeit a substantial minority (35 per cent), think that people go so far as to neglect their health because the NHS is there to pick up the pieces. More (45 per cent) feel that such behaviour does not exist. Again, DEs are more cynical than ABs in this respect.[3]

Asked to say from a list of three possibilities how the NHS should be funded, most (55 per cent) at that time opted for increasing taxes; 20 per cent favoured maintaining current levels of taxation but increasing the level of rationing; slightly fewer (16 per cent) said they would favour cutting taxes while encouraging

---

3   Ibid., pp. 42–3.

individuals to take out private medical insurance.[4] Significantly, the study found that:

> Those especially likely to favour the introduction of rationing in return for no increase in taxation are those from the lowest social classes and aged under 25 (36 per cent), and those aged over 25 who are frequent users of health services (29 per cent). Conversely, few ABC1s aged 35+ feel that this would be the best way forward (11 per cent).[5]

Two-thirds of respondents (65 per cent) said that a health service paid for by taxes should be free at the point of use for everyone. Almost one in five (17 per cent) felt that the NHS should charge everyone, except those most in need. And a similar number (16 per cent) were in favour of a sliding scale of charges based on income:

> Asked, which of these three options is most likely to exist in the Britain of 2007, the majority of adults feel some kind of payment will be required. A mere one in eight (13 per cent) envisage that a service that is free at the point of delivery, much like the NHS of today, will still be in place.[6]

When it came to rationing:

> Two thirds (67 per cent) of adults think that the NHS of 2007 will provide fewer services than the NHS of today and that certain services will only be available privately. Far fewer think this scenario unlikely (18 per cent), and 14 per cent have no strong opinion either way. The very old and the very young are among the least inclined to think that the NHS will not provide as many services in ten years' time,

4   Ibid., pp. 48–9.

5   Ibid., p. 48.

6   Ibid., pp. 54–5.

although even among these groups the majority anticipate reduced provision.[7]

Overall, an evaluation of the data:

> … shows the disparity between expectations and desire, and arguably between reality and wishes. Although widely expected, such a change would clearly be unpopular. Four out of five adults say they would oppose a reduction in the number of services provided by the NHS, compared with just one-tenth who would be supportive.[8]

As well as expecting fewer services to be available, the public also expected to see an increase in service rationing. In total, three-quarters (76 per cent) of the adults surveyed believed the amount of prioritising would have increased in a decade. Just one tenth expected the opposite. Most (62 per cent) adults thought that NHS services would no longer be free at the point of use by 2007. Here:

> Age has a marked impact on perception. Young people (15–24) are much more likely than older people (55+) to expect that payment will be required for NHS services … Clearly, such expectation is not based on public longing. The vast majority (four in five) oppose the principle of paying to use NHS services. By contrast, just one in eight (12 per cent) are supportive (a mere 1 per cent strongly so).[9]

Respondents widely anticipated that the proportion of individuals with private medical insurance (PMI) would be greater in ten years' time than it was at the time of the survey: 'Eight in ten expect

---

7   Ibid., p. 54.

8   Ibid.

9   Ibid., p. 64.

to see an increase in the proportion of individuals who have voluntarily taken out PMI, compared with just 8 per cent who think that an increase is unlikely.'[10] Some 53 per cent of respondents said they would support an increase in the proportion of adults voluntarily taking out PMI and 18 per cent said they would be opposed. Again, when it came to questions of quality of treatment:

> Opinion is divided over whether the quality of treatment offered by the NHS in any way differs from the quality of treatment provided by private suppliers. Four in ten think that the two services are about equal, three in ten think that private care has the edge, and one in ten perceive the NHS to be superior.[11]

Again, however, age has a considerable impact on perception. Younger people were much more likely to be advocates of private treatment than their older counterparts.

Overall, the implications of this groundbreaking research are clear. As Bosanquet and Pollard concluded:

> The summary indicates that the public is beginning to accept that change is inevitable. Some groups appear more receptive to change than others, implying that they may be willing to consider yet more reform, or that they may serve to influence other elements of society. However, it should be appreciated that (in most cases) only a minority in each group actively welcomes reform.[12]

Although public opinion is today evidently in a very different world from that into which the NHS was born, the MORI research clearly indicates a central contradiction in popular perception.

---

10   Ibid., p. 84.
11   Ibid., p. 90.
12   Ibid., p. 93.

The most striking general finding of the survey is the gap between expectations and wants. Broadly, the public wants the NHS to offer everything, and to offer it free; 65 per cent say, for instance, the NHS services would always be free. But, crucially, a mere 13 per cent expect that they will be free in ten years' time. Some 67 per cent think that the NHS will provide fewer services and that those no longer covered will only be available privately, even though 80 per cent do not like such a prospect.[13]

Elite opinion formation

Nigel Lawson stated in 1992 that: 'The National Health Service is the closest thing the English have to a religion, with those who practise in it regarding themselves as a priesthood.'[14] While it is always difficult to prove a causal relationship between opinion formers such as journalists, academics, politicians, government officials, members of interest groups, and the widely held beliefs of ordinary citizens, there nevertheless do exist in society views that are popular and widespread at any point in time. In many instances, the job of the social scientist is to examine such beliefs, and to provide more powerful explanations of their nature and boundaries than would otherwise be afforded from everyday, commonsense, interpretation.

As such, the research that lies at the heart of this work is concerned with those leading opinion formers who interpret, guide and report on the NHS – and healthcare more generally – on a day-to-day basis. In exploring their understanding of health economics and such notions as market failure,

13   Ibid., pp. 98–9.
14   Nigel Lawson, *The View from Number Eleven*, Doubleday, London, 1992.

government failure and market success, the limits and boundaries of current discourse can be identified, clarified and ultimately challenged.

In Britain today, journalists, academics, politicians, government officials and members of health interest groups wield substantial power and influence over the way health policy and delivery are reported and discussed.

The media

The British national press is one of the most pervasive in the world, attracting a comparatively high percentage of readers. It boasts no fewer than twenty (general) daily and Sunday titles[15] and, at the dawn of the 21st century, just five groups control over four-fifths of national circulation.[16] Remarkably: 'No new national newspaper launched in the last eighty years has been able to stay independent.'[17]

Journalists in the national press, and on television and radio, have an enormous role to play when it comes to the articulation of health policy options and wider public opinion. For some authors power relations in a liberal corporatist society mean that:

> ... a consensus is formed through consultation between
> government and organized interests. The system is 'liberal'
> in the sense that political parties tend to alternate, the
> armed forces are firmly under the control of civil authority
> and freedoms are not undermined by coercive measures.

15   This excludes the *Sport* and *Sunday Sport*. This figure also excludes the *Morning Star* because it is rarely stocked by newsagents and is therefore not nationally available.

16   J. Curran, *Media and Power*, Routledge, London, 2002, p. 231.

17   Ibid.

> But within this system, the consensus of society tends to be defined by the major players ... [18]

For Curran and Seaton, the British national press puts forward a relatively narrow and an essentially corporatist view of the world. They comment: 'The national press has reproduced a remarkably narrow arc of opinion, indeed sometimes only one opinion, in its editorials on a range of issues.'[19]

Whereas conservative orthodoxy portrays the media as reflecting and serving society, and its more libertarian counterparts maintain that the media is implicated in the management of society, this study remains essentially neutral on such questions of societal power. It is simply not within its purview to examine power relations between the organised media, ordinary people in society and their complex interactions.

Whether the media reflects or manages public opinion on health issues is, in many ways, irrelevant for the purposes of this study. What matters instead is the nature, profile and boundaries of the dominant worldview. That is, the widely held views and beliefs of opinion formers on the problems and possibilities for health policy and health delivery.

Academia

Today in Britain there are more than 2,800 higher education courses offered in more than 150 universities, colleges, insti-

---

18   Ibid., pp. 231–2.
19   See J. Curran and J. Seaton, *Power without Responsibility: The Press and Broadcasting in Britain*, 5th edn, Routledge, London, 1997.

tutes and conservatoires.[20] More than 40 per cent of school leavers now continue on into higher education – and by 2010 the government wants more than 50 per cent of school leavers to participate in degree courses.[21] Dr Madsen Pirie of the Adam Smith Institute suggests that the impact that these institutions and courses have on students and wider opinion is not to be underestimated:

> … You pack up for life while you are at university or college and the goods you take on board have to sustain you through the journey. Very few people make major intellectual changes during the course of their adult lives, so obviously what is done in the universities is very important for the future …[22]

Similarly, Dennis O'Keeffe and David Marsland conclude their work *Independence or Stagnation? The Imperatives of University Reform in the United Kingdom*: 'British higher education is by far the most promising place to begin the course of necessary economic and intellectual correction.'[23]

The power of government

In 2006/07, British government spending accounted for more than 45 per cent of gross domestic product (GDP). Expenditure on the NHS and personal social services accounts for a sizeable share of planned government expenditure. Total government spending on

---

20 Lee Elliot Major, 'Armed with the facts', *Guardian*, 28 May 2002.
21 Polly Curtis, 'University applications recover from slump', *Guardian*, 18 July 2003.
22 Dr Madsen Pirie in a recorded interview.
23 D. O'Keefe and D. Marsland, *Independence or Stagnation? The Imperatives of University Reform in the United Kingdom*, CIVITAS, London, 2003, p. 63.

the NHS is expected to be £90 billion in the current fiscal year and is projected to rise by 4 per cent in real terms in each of the next two years. Not included in this figure is spending on personal social services, which is approximately 20 per cent of the level of NHS spending, so that, overall, in 2007/08, the state is spending about £110 billion on health and social care. Back in 2002, the government announced plans for UK spending on health to rise by 7.2 per cent in real terms up to the year 2007/08.[24] Though this has not quite been achieved, real spending has risen very rapidly in the last five years.

The NHS, personal social services and the Department of Health employ more than one million people. Many tens of thousands more work in a wide range of other health interests closely aligned to the state. Groups include such organisations as the Health and Safety Executive (HSE), Action on Smoking and Health (ASH) and the medical Royal Colleges. All receive state funding, or legislative favour, or both.

The new class health nexus

In many ways today's senior managers in and around the state's health nexus hold characteristics and qualities similar to those first identified by the proponents of New Class theory. Although far broader in scope than healthcare, the idea of a New Class was originally put forward by Daniel Bell in his book *The Coming of the Post-Industrial Society*.[25]

Bell essentially argued then that developed nations were on the verge of a post-industrial society in which the production and distribution of knowledge would replace the production and

24   HM Treasury, *2002 Chancellor's Budget*.
25   D. Bell, *The Coming of the Post-Industrial Society*, Basic Books, New York, 1976.

distribution of goods as the dominant activity of society:

> Just as the business firm was the key institution of the past
> hundred years because of its role in organising production
> for the mass creation of products, the university will become
> the central institution of the next hundred years because of
> its role as the new source of innovation and knowledge.[26]

At its heart, the New Class has three common features, as Nigel Ashford has commented: 'Firstly, they belong to a common occupational strata, related to knowledge and ideas. Secondly, they share a set of common values, towards economics, politics and culture. Thirdly, they have a common interest in expanding the public sector.'[27]

It was Joseph Schumpeter who argued that intellectuals: '… develop group attitudes and group interests sufficiently strong to make large numbers of them behave in a way that is usually associated with the concept of social classes'.[28]

For Irving Kristol, members of the New Class can be found in a detailed and specific list. They include:

> Scientists, teachers and educational administrators,
> journalists and others in the communications industries,
> psychologists, social workers, those lawyers and doctors
> who make their careers in the expanding public sector, city
> planners, the staffs of large foundations, the upper level of
> the government bureaucracy and so on.[29]

---

26 Ibid., p. 343.
27 N. Ashford, *Neo-Conservatism and the New Class: A Critical Evaluation*, Sociological Notes no. 3, Libertarian Alliance, London, 1986, p. 2.
28 J. Schumpeter, *Capitalism, Socialism and Democracy*, Allen & Unwin, London, 1942, p. 134.
29 I. Kristol, *Two Cheers for Capitalism*, Basic Books, New York, 1978, p. 27.

To proponents of New Class theory, its most important members are academics, for they act as the prime legitimators of society. Academics have great power because of their direct contact with students and because they produce ideas consumed by other members of the New Class. Importantly, academics act as a reference group for the other factions within the New Class who do not have the time or capacity to develop their own ideas.

In the 1970s, Lipset found that the incidence of leftism was associated with being an academic professor and in particular a social scientist. Professors and university lecturers were far more likely to describe themselves as liberal (in the American sense) or radical than any other group in society. Social scientists, with their potential for a more direct impact upon public policy, were more left wing and statist than those from other disciplines.[30] Similarly, David Marsland argued in his book *Seeds of Bankruptcy: Sociological Bias against Business and Freedom* that British sociology and its practitioners in the main have been captured by a statist, anti-enterprise, anti-freedom mindset.[31]

Another major group employed in the New Class is those involved in journalism. Today, an overwhelming majority of journalists are university graduates. As a result of their education – and their desire to achieve and sustain their high status – they look to academics as an important reference group: 'So that comments from academics are almost obligatory in the quality newspapers and magazines.'[32]

---

30 In the US context, 76 per cent voted for George McGovern as President and 64 per cent identified themselves as being liberal or very liberal.

31 D. Marsland, *Seeds of Bankruptcy: Sociological Bias against Business and Freedom*, Claridge Press, London, 1988.

32 E. C. Ladd and S. Lipset, *The Divided Academy*, Norton, New York, 1975; S. Lipset and R. Dobson, 'The intellectual as critic and rebel', *Daedalus*, 101(3): 211–89.

Members of the New Class are also found among government officials, public sector employees (such as schoolteachers and social workers) and in key professions such as law and medicine.

The New Class thus represents a substantial number of people in modern Britain and across the West. But even more important than their numbers is their position in the strategically important sectors of modern society. In the economic sphere the New Class is thought to be essentially socialist – not in terms of formally advocating the state ownership of the means of production, but in its concerns with the distribution of income and wealth arising from the market. Ashford explains it in the following terms:

> The New Class want the distribution of income to be determined by the principle of social justice, which means by their contribution to society determined collectively. However, such a position assumes that someone knows what is socially just, and has the authority to distribute income on those principles. Distribution would be determined by the state, over which the New Class has so much influence, rather than by the market, where there are only a minority of consumers.[33]

Similarly, Irving Kristol has commented: 'There is a class of people who believe that they can define "social justice", that they have an authoritative conception of the common good that should be imposed on society by using the force of government.'[34]

Arguably, one key source of power for the New Class is a lack of opposition to its ideas. One possible source of opposition might come from the business community. Indeed, Kristol argues that there is a form of class war being waged between the New Class

---

33   Ashford, op. cit., p. 4.
34   Kristol, op. cit., p. 67.

and those in business. The latter lack an appropriate response and strategy, however, because they simply do not possess the necessary political and tactical skills to fight back.[35] Furthermore, increasing acceptance of concepts such as corporate social responsibility[36] undermines the proft-maximising and wealth-creating functions of business in favour of a corporatism that can be directed and manipulated by members of the New Class: 'The relative weakness of the business class in the field of ideas and symbols, as compared with the massive strength of the New Class in precisely these areas, has significantly altered the power relationship between the two elites.'[37]

Given such evidence, it is at least plausible that the leading opinion formers in the worlds of British health journalism, academia, politics, government and interest groups will have a disproportionately high impact on the way the NHS, healthcare and health policy are thought about in wider society. In exploring their understanding of health economics and such notions as market failure, government failure and market success, one should be able to highlight and examine some of the limits, boundaries and biases of popular discourse and opinion.

Shifting ground among elite opinion

Since 1997 it could be argued that the government has exploited the public's 'dampened expectations' on healthcare and, as such, ministers have been able to move forward with incremental

---

35 Ibid. See also M. Bruce-Riggs (ed.), *The New Class*, Transaction Books, New Brunswick, NJ, 1979, ch. 5.

36 Ashford, op. cit., p. 7.

37 M. Novak, *The American Vision*, American Enterprise Institute, Washington, DC, 1978, p. 34.

elements of a market-oriented approach. As has been stated previously, acceptance of public–private partnerships, the 2000 Concordat with independent hospitals, the arrival of Foundation Trusts (albeit in a watered down form of what was initially envisaged) and the arrival of Independent Sector Treatment Centres all conspire to suggest a government at ease with elements of non-state provision.

As such, today's political class are starting to leave the NHS's vision and promises of the 1940s behind. Instead of seeing the service in its fully nationalised format, politicians are busy recasting it as a regulator and a funder of healthcare but not necessarily the owner or manager of the facilities in which healthcare is actually delivered.

Similarly, while they see the government remaining a key funder of healthcare they ultimately see it only as one of a number. With millions of people already covered by private medical insurance, private cash plans or willing to self-fund, it is perhaps no surprise that even back in 1997 53 per cent of respondents said they would support an increase in the proportion of adults voluntarily taking out private health cover.[38] Nevertheless, this does not necessarily mean that anything like a genuine free market is becoming accepted by opinion formers or the electorate.

Ever since Roman times, political elites in Britain have always sought to plan, control and regulate the provision of health services. Through the Roman military, the Christian church, the Royal Colleges, Parliament, and the timeless granting of legislative favour, the state has always sought to empire-build and to control people's access to healthcare and medicine. Far from operating

---

38 Bosanquet and Pollard, op. cit., p. 88.

in a genuine market, healthcare has always been a highly politicised and controlled activity: one that rests in large measure on
coercion and government licence. As such, the principles of a
genuine market have never been applied to this most important
area of human activity.

Importance of language

Indeed, the way that the language of the market is often applied
to the analysis of health policy is itself a highly questionable and
potentially damaging practice. For if the language and notions
of the market are imputed to describe what are in reality identified problems that have more to do with state interventionism
and government failure, the entire debate becomes set on a
highly confused and ultimately meaningless linguistic foundation. If the language and phraseology of the market are invoked to
describe particular institutions that have failed, yet the structures,
incentives and reality of healthcare remain essentially statist,
public discourse runs the risk of being completely distorted and
prejudiced.

On the popular question of externalities, for instance, while
the genuine believer in free markets might seek reform by the
internalisation of externalities, the unintelligible relativist might
genuinely believe that externalities are an inevitable outcome of
what is already popularly accepted as a market. To put it another
way: if a market is not rigorously adhered to in terms of such
operational definitions as private property rights, the rule of law
and market-driven reputation then it cannot be said in any meaningful sense to be a genuine market. If a General Medical Council,
a Royal College or a private company is granted legislative favour

by the state, then it can no longer be said to be *of the market* in any objective and meaningful sense.

Arguably, in a genuine market, the providers of health would have to succumb to the rigours of consumer power and the levelling principles of arbitrage. Could it be that the reason why professionals receive more than 40 per cent more NHS spending per illness episode than those on lower incomes is not (in causal terms) because the middle classes are better at asserting their rights, but instead because such built-in inequity is the inevitable product of the political economy of legislative favour, professional monopoly and producer capture?

In the following chapters we will present and analyse a study of elite opinion of the NHS and alternative forms of health provision. The research that lies at the heart of this analysis is seeking to find out how British opinion formers, at the beginning of the 21st century, think about markets in healthcare and to what extent they adhere to a rigorous and logical analysis.

When a representative sample of leading health opinion formers – journalists, academics, politicians, government officials and members of relevant interest groups – think about 'a free market in health', what meaning does such a notion have for them? What is their perspective on what a market in health is or could be? We will see how their thinking about a free market is distorted by the language of the debate.

Ultimately, in surveying respondents' views and assessing relevant commonalities and cleavages in their attitudes, the study aims to profile and assess the limits, boundaries and biases of this influential group's beliefs and suppositions.

5 AN INQUIRY INTO ELITE OPINION ON NOTIONS OF MARKET FAILURE AND STATE FAILURE IN HEALTH ECONOMICS

Key propositions of the market failure paradigm

As David Green has quite rightly pointed out: 'The dominant academic view is that attempts by ordinary people to obtain health care for themselves, without the help of the state, are bound to suffer from a number of serious "market failures".'[1] It is the contention of the research that lies at the heart of this work that there are six primary biases, limits and self-imposed boundaries that currently guide the beliefs of health opinion formers.

The first is the concept of *monopoly*. It is commonly assumed that a health market is particularly vulnerable to monopoly and producer capture. Instead of seeing these traits as the weaknesses of statism and political culture, however, it is an a priori belief among opinion formers that medical professions will be able to gain legislative favour and organise against the consumer to raise prices and to minimise accountability for medical wrongdoing. Crucially, the idea of precluding such legislative favour and of consumers becoming reliant on market-borne reputation (as opposed to regulation) is simply not articulated. One of the ironies of the monopoly debate in health (and in other markets) is that those who often appear to be most concerned about it invariably

---

1   D. Green, *Working Class Patients and the Medical Establishment*, Gower, Aldershot, 1985, p. 3.

suggest that it should be the greatest monopolist of them all – the state – which is used to deal with the assumed problems to which monopoly gives rise.

The second issue is *consumer ignorance*. It is commonly held that because of his superior knowledge, the doctor will always face the consumer as the dominant party, and that this will be a problem made worse by medical advance. Here there appears to be little understanding or empathy for the view that brands, reputation and third-party assessments, essential institutions in a free society, can overcome many of the problems associated with consumer ignorance. There is little faith in the idea that the market would discover over time means and mechanisms that would empower and embolden the consumer. Again, the idea that state monopoly or regulation would in any way empower the consumer more than a genuine market is an interesting yet highly questionable notion.

The third area of popular concern is *neglect of the poor and chronically sick*. Here, it is believed that even if the market does not wholly neglect the poor and chronically sick, they would inevitably receive an altogether inferior service to that provided by the state. Instead of seeing the market as an instrument that offers built-in incentives to level social power and encourage greater prosperity for the benefit and inclusion of all, it is seen as a divisive mechanism that perpetuates exclusion and poverty. It is rarely asserted that the state neglects the poor and the chronically sick, despite the evidence presented above, as a result of the poor having a less effective 'voice' in the political and bureaucratic process that leads to state-provided healthcare. Again, as Hayek, Mises and Rothbard suggest, there is little understanding that, in a real market, new and innovative enterprises and brands would emerge to deal with such vulnerable groups through ways that we have not yet discovered.

The fourth area is *externalities*. It is widely believed that there are negative externalities or third-party effects requiring government regulation, notably that the doctor and the patient may ignore the exposure of others to such factors as contagious disease. Here it is popularly assumed that a state will respond faster and more effectively to an external problem than a genuine market. Two points should be noted. First, the existence of externality is a symptom of a market that is not complete. The situation may be improved by government intervention but the first question that should be asked is whether there is an alternative way of internalising social costs. Second, government health provision itself creates enormous externalities because of the absence of differential premiums for individuals with different habits and lifestyles.

The fifth area is a lack of provision of *public goods*. Under this argument it is held that some healthcare is a 'public good' and as such it must be supplied by government. Perhaps the most popular reason for seeing health as a public good is the idea that only government can effectively manage and eliminate an outbreak of a contagious disease. Instead of arguing that the market would itself create effective mechanisms and means to deal with such a situation, government is viewed a priori as the only agency capable of effective management. Importantly, when it comes to the public goods debate, there is little questioning of the capacity for politicians to cover up, deny, obfuscate, misdirect or mismanage – not least because government invariably lacks the sophisticated means by which vital evaluations and assessments can be encouraged.

The final argument popularly invoked relates to the apparent problems of the *perverse incentives of insurance.* Here, it is argued that demand for healthcare is more uncertain than for most other products and in practice this has meant that insurance has played a major role in healthcare funding. As such, it is said that there are special difficulties with health insurance. Once a person is covered by insurance he has a reduced incentive to avoid health-care costs. Similarly, once premiums have been paid the individual has an incentive to initiate the delivery of healthcare: that is, to 'get his money's worth'. Finally, where a third party does not control payment, the doctor or the patient may have an incentive not to contain costs. In all of this, there has been scant regard for the perverse incentives of state healthcare. Just because the demand for healthcare might be more uncertain than for some other products it does not necessary follow that government is better placed to deal with this than powerful consumers in real markets.

Again, while it is popularly assumed that insurance is the private model of choice, it remains possible that in a real market other arrangements might become the norm. For example, it is often said that in a free market many uninsured motor accident victims would simply be left to die by the side of the road. But would this really happen? Would a market not develop whereby some health providers offered free rescue and medical treatment provided the victim signed up to a health plan for a specified period? After all, this is precisely how many motor vehicle accident organisations such as the Automobile Association and the Royal Automobile Club deal with a vehicle breakdown now.

Also, is it not true that once a person has been promised free and unlimited healthcare by a government this reduces the incentive to avoid healthcare costs? Once taxes have been paid and the government has made this promise, do not individuals have an incentive to initiate the delivery of healthcare and to 'get what is theirs by right'? Finally, why would it be assumed that in a real market the doctor or the patient would not have adequate incentives to contain costs? Surely, that is what markets arrange in and of themselves? The suggestion that governments (as third-party payers) can better ensure such an efficient outcome is surely a highly questionable and contentious proposition.

Approach to qualitative research

While one of the key teachings of social science is that we are all ultimately bound by the beliefs and epistemology of our age, it is nevertheless, as Anthony Giddens has so powerfully argued,[2] a primary function of those formally engaged in social enquiry to challenge and expose the boundaries, inconsistencies and contexts in which worldviews become accepted and are ultimately internalised. It is possible that the long-held and widely held views above are gradually shifting. It is the purpose of this study to understand better the views of key opinion formers about governments and markets in health.

In exploring the underlying beliefs and values of health opinion formers in the context of how they think about notions of market failure and market success, it was decided early on that such an enquiry would be suitable for qualitative research. The research data was gathered through telephone interviews with each respondent. Containing a series of questions that explored the respondent's values, ideas and notions surrounding such areas

---

2   Anthony Giddens, *New Rules of Sociological Methodology*, Hutchinson, London, 1976.

as monopoly, consumer ignorance, neglect of the poor and chronically sick, externalities, public goods, and perverse incentives, a subsequent analysis of the data facilitated insights into the nature and degree of the boundaries and intellectual limits that opinion formers currently set.

Although social enquiry is never value free, research in the form of a telephone interview questionnaire does facilitate a certain degree of dispassionate objectivity. Through the setting of methodologically appropriate questions, a number of statistical tools can be applied which in turn help to interpret and contextualise the insights gained. To further aid analysis, the research has also been enhanced by a series of open-ended questions towards the end of each telephone interview.

Given the subject matter and the constraints of undertaking this research, it is inevitable that the data and information achieved would have to be interpreted to some extent. But in view of the powerful results obtained and outlined below, it is only fair to say that the explanations provided are not a matter of subjective, personal opinion, but instead accurately reflect the values, beliefs and boundaries of the population concerned.

The sample

The sample for this study covers the influential worlds of journalism, academia, politics, civil service and key interest groups. For reasons of definitional complexity and because of the sensitivity of the research (not least for reasons of individual confidentiality), it was not possible to examine a perfectly random sample. Nevertheless, the research compiled is from an accurate and representative sample of leading national newspaper, electronic media, party political, civil service and health interest group commentators.

It is estimated that out of the leading national newspapers, the author questioned more than 90 per cent of currently serving and recent health correspondents. Ten leading national health journalists were interviewed (see Table 1). Concerning the electronic media, ten leading health correspondents and journalists from the BBC, Independent Television News and Sky News were interviewed.

Similarly, ten leading health and social policy academics were interviewed. All of them work in some of Britain's most respected university departments, have written several books on healthcare and social policy, and/or regularly appear as commentators on health in the press and media.

In politics, a sample of ten past and current health spokesmen were interviewed from the country's main political parties – Labour, Conservative and Liberal Democrat – including those ranked at ministerial, junior ministerial and backbench levels. To further strengthen the parliamentary sample ten past and present members of the House of Commons Health Select Committee were interviewed. To access party policy expertise, ten party political advisers and researchers on health policy and social policy were interviewed. Concerning the civil service, ten senior officials from the Department of Health and other key ministries – such as the Treasury – were interviewed.

Ten senior respondents were interviewed from a wide range of health interest groups. These included respondents from the General Medical Council, the British Medical Association, a selection of Royal Medical Colleges, leading health trade unions, private sector organisations, charities and patients' groups.

Also, ten leading public policy thinkers from a selection of think tanks and ten senior medical and health professionals were interviewed.

Table 1 **Definition of interviewees**

Sample frame	Number of respondents
1 Newspaper health journalists	10
2 Electronic media health journalists	10
3 Health and social policy academics	10
4 Party political health spokesmen	10
5 Members of the House of Commons Health Select Committee	10
6 Party political advisers on health and social policy	10
7 Senior civil servants	10
8 Health interest groups	10
9 Think tanks	10
10 Senior medical and health professionals	10

In total, 100 leading health commentators were surveyed, making this the largest ever analysis of notions of health market failure and success among influential British opinion formers. From the outset, respondents were told that the information gathered was for academic research concerned with the analysis of notions of market failure and success in healthcare.

Given the political sensitivities surrounding this subject, the respondents were assured that their anonymity would be guaranteed at all times and that their identities would not be revealed. Throughout the process, it was made clear that the respondents' own personal views were required. As such, 'don't know' (DK) options were not included in the quantitative research because, as Schuman and Presser advise, in a survey

such as this, which is interested in people's underlying disposi-
tions, it is better to encourage a definite 'one way or the other'
response by not providing a 'get out'.[3]

Overall, as will be seen later, there was an unusually low level
of non-response. The data achieved was generated from 100 per
cent of the initial sample frame.

Important research

This research is of fundamental importance because it seeks to
illuminate the boundaries, limits and presumptions upon which
one of the most important debates in modern British society is
conducted. The discourse surrounding the economics and politics
of healthcare is not, however, simply relevant to Britain and the
National Health Service. It has wider global implications that
potentially impact on the lives of millions of people in both the
developed and the underdeveloped world.

Today Britain remains one of the largest economies in the
world. It is one of the world's leading industrial nations. And its
economic, military and cultural prowess carries huge international
weight and influence. As a world connected in real time increasingly speaks English as its international language, then health
policy in Britain really does matter. For, while during the first six
decades of the twentieth century, British Fabian socialists sought
to export their ideas on health, welfare and economics to foreign
and Commonwealth nations around the world,[4] Britain's policy

---

3   H. Schuman and S. Presser, *Questions and Answers in Attitude Surveys*, Academic
     Press, New York, 1981.
4   Donald F. Butsky, *Democratic Socialism: A Global Survey*, Praeger, Westport, CT,
     2000.

exporters now seem to have become the primary champions of a new corporatist project: namely, public–private partnerships.

In the broader political, economic and cultural context, the way leading British health opinion formers think about health-care, and the economic rubrics that of necessity underpin it, is of huge significance.

For as the 21st century opens up before us and the world of healthcare leaves behind the model of full-blown nationalisation, the question arises as to what will replace it. If its emergent demise suggests a transition or a vacuum, what will be the underlying principles that guide market-inclined reform?

In the future, will opinion formers continue to perpetuate historical notions of market failure in healthcare or give new voice to notions of government failure? When it comes to markets in health, is there intellectual scope among opinion formers for embracing notions of market success?

6 IDEAS OF MARKET FAILURE AND GOVERNMENT FAILURE AMONG BRITISH HEALTH OPINION FORMERS

Research findings

As was made clear in the previous chapter, the research that lies at the heart of this study centred on a telephone interview and questionnaire, finally completed via a cross-checking process in 2007. Overall, 100 respondents were chosen in the sample frame, ten from each of the following categories of opinion former: newspaper health journalists, electronic media health journalists, health and social policy academics, party political health spokesmen, members of the House of Commons Health Select Committee, party political advisers on health and social policy, senior civil servants, health interest groups, think tank policy experts, senior medical and health professionals.

Significantly, 100 per cent of the respondents fully participated in the research. Together, they account for a high percentage of British health opinion formers and as such the data generated can be said to have a high degree of external validity.

The survey itself was divided into three sections. The first section (Section A) dealt with 'Opinions towards market failure in healthcare' and the second (Section B) concentrated on 'Opinions towards government failure in healthcare'. The third section (Section C) concerned general 'Parameters in the health-care debate'. In total, there were 21 questions with seven in section A (1–7), seven in section B (8–14) and seven in section C (15–21).

Opinions on 'market failure'

Questions 1 to 7 invited respondents to agree or disagree with particular statements. For each question, respondents were given the following instruction: 'On a scale of 1–10, with 1 being "strongly disagree" and 10 being "strongly agree", can you please tell me what you think of the following statement?'

Table 2 **Views on the problem of monopoly**

Q.A1 'If a real market in healthcare existed, government would still have to intervene to stop problems of monopoly.'

	1	2	3	4	5	6	7	8	9	10	Avg.
Newspaper health journalists	0	0	0	0	2	2	3	2	1	0	5.4
Electronic media health journalists	1	0	2	0	2	0	0	2	0	3	6.3
Health and social policy academics	4	0	1	1	0	1	0	2	0	1	4.3
Party political health spokesmen	1	2	1	0	1	0	2	1	2	0	5.3
Members of the H of C HSC	0	0	0	1	1	2	0	2	2	2	7.5
Party political advisers	0	0	1	1	1	1	1	4	0	1	6.7
Senior civil servants	0	2	3	0	0	1	0	0	1	3	5.6
Health interest group representatives	0	0	1	0	0	1	3	1	0	4	7.8
Think tank policy experts	2	2	1	0	1	0	0	3	1	0	4.7
Senior medical and health professionals	1	0	1	1	3	0	2	2	0	0	5.3
Totals	9	6	11	4	11	8	11	19	7	14	
Overall average 5.9											

In response to the statement 'If a real market in healthcare existed, government would still have to intervene to stop problems of monopoly' all respondent categories answered within the (slightly negative) 4.3 to (reasonably positive) 7.8 range. Overall, the opinion-forming 100 averaged a score of 5.9. The detailed results are shown in Table 2.

Nevertheless, below this headline average there were some important differences. While health interest group representatives (7.8), party political advisers (6.7) and electronic media journalists (6.3) tended to agree with the view that government would have to stop problems of monopoly, there was clearly more caution from the health and social policy academics (4.3) and the think tank policy experts (4.7). The latter appeared to be much more questioning of the notion of monopoly and somewhat sceptical of the benefits of government intervention.

Table 3 **Views on consumer ignorance**

Q.A2 'If a real market in healthcare existed, government would still have to intervene to provide objective information to overcome problems of consumer ignorance'.

	1	2	3	4	5	6	7	8	9	10	Avg.
Newspaper health journalists	0	0	2	0	0	0	5	0	2	1	6.9
Electronic media health journalists	0	0	0	0	2	1	2	1	1	3	7.7
Health and social policy academics	4	0	0	0	0	1	0	2	0	3	5.6
Party political health spokesmen	0	1	1	0	0	2	3	2	1	0	6.3
Members of the H of C HSC	0	0	1	1	0	0	3	2	3	0	7.1
Party political advisers	0	0	3	2	0	1	1	0	0	2	5.0
Senior civil servants	2	0	2	3	0	0	1	2	0	0	4.3
Health interest group representatives	0	1	0	0	2	1	0	2	0	4	7.4
Think tank policy experts	4	1	1	1	1	0	2	0	0	0	3.2
Senior medical and health professionals	1	0	1	3	0	1	1	3	0	0	5.3
Totals	11	3	11	10	5	7	18	14	7	14	
Overall average 5.8											

In response to the statement 'If a real market in healthcare existed, government would still have to intervene to provide objective information to overcome problems of consumer ignorance' all respondent categories answered within the relatively wide (negative) 3.2 to (reasonably positive) 7.7 range. Overall, the opinion-forming 100 averaged a score of 5.8; see Table 3.

Again, looking beyond the average, there are some important differences. While electronic media health journalists (7.7), health interest group representatives (7.4) and newspaper health journalists (6.9) tended to agree with the view that government would have to provide objective information to overcome problems of consumer ignorance, there was clear scepticism from the think tank policy experts (3.2). This latter group appeared to be not only more questioning of the notion of objective information per se but were sceptical of it when its codification and dissemination were attempted through government intervention.

Table 4 **Protecting the poor and chronically sick**

Q.A3 'If a real market in healthcare existed, government would still have to intervene to protect the poor and chronically sick from neglect.'

	1	2	3	4	5	6	7	8	9	10	Avg.
Newspaper health journalists	0	0	0	0	0	1	2	1	3	3	8.5
Electronic media health journalists	0	0	0	0	0	0	1	0	2	7	9.5
Health and social policy academics	2	1	0	0	2	0	1	0	1	3	6.0
Party political health spokesmen	1	0	0	0	0	1	1	3	2	2	7.6
Members of the H of C HSC	0	0	0	0	0	0	2	1	1	6	9.1
Party political advisers	0	0	1	1	1	1	2	1	0	3	7.0
Senior civil servants	2	0	0	2	1	0	2	1	0	2	5.7
Health interest group representatives	0	0	0	1	0	0	2	1	1	5	8.5
Think tank policy experts	2	1	1	0	1	1	0	1	1	2	5.5
Senior medical and health professionals	1	0	1	1	0	2	1	3	1	0	6.0
Totals	8	2	3	5	5	6	14	12	12	33	

Overall average 7.3

In response to the statement 'If a real market in healthcare existed, government would still have to intervene to protect the poor and chronically sick from neglect' all respondent categories answered within the (neutral) 5.5 to (very positive) 9.5 range. Overall, the opinion-forming 100 averaged a reasonably positive score of 7.3. The results are summarised in Table 4.

While electronic media health journalists (9.5), health interest group representatives (8.5) and newspaper health journalists (8.5) tended to agree with the view that government would have to intervene to protect the poor and chronically sick from neglect, there was a seemingly neutral scepticism from the think tank policy experts (5.5), senior civil servants (5.7), health and social policy academics (6.0) and senior medical and health professionals (6.0). The think tank policy experts, civil servants and health and social policy academics were at best neutral towards the idea of government interventionism benefiting the poor and chronically sick. The similarly neutral stance of the senior medical and health professionals may have come from the perspective that they – not central government – are best placed to help the poor and chronically sick.

Table 5 **Is government policy necessary to protect people from contagious disease?**

Q.A4 'If a real market in healthcare existed, government would still have to intervene to help protect people from such external factors as contagious disease.'

	1	2	3	4	5	6	7	8	9	10	Avg.
Newspaper health journalists	0	0	0	0	1	0	1	1	2	5	8.8
Electronic media health journalists	0	1	0	0	0	0	0	1	2	6	8.8
Health and social policy academics	0	2	1	0	1	0	0	2	1	3	6.7
Party political health spokesmen	0	1	0	0	0	0	2	1	1	5	8.3
Members of the H of C HSC	0	0	0	0	0	0	0	2	2	6	9.4
Party political advisers	0	0	3	0	0	1	0	1	1	4	7.2
Senior civil servants	0	0	2	1	0	0	3	0	1	3	7.0
Health interest group representatives	0	0	0	0	0	0	3	1	1	5	8.8
Think tank policy experts	0	1	0	0	4	1	1	2	0	1	6.1
Senior medical and health professionals	1	0	1	2	2	1	1	1	0	1	5.3
Totals	1	5	7	3	8	3	11	12	11	39	

Overall average 7.6

In response to the statement 'If a real market in healthcare existed, government would still have to intervene to protect people from such external factors as contagious disease' all respondent categories answered within the (neutral) 5.3 to (very positive) 9.4 range. Overall, the opinion-forming 100 averaged a positive score of 7.6 (Table 5).

Again, there were important differences within the sample. While members of the House of Commons Health Select Committee (9.4), electronic media health journalists (8.8), newspaper health journalists (8.8) and health interest group representatives (8.8) stood out as tending to agree strongly with the view that government would have to protect people from such external factors as contagious disease, there was a more neutral stance from the senior medical and health professionals (5.3) and the think tank policy experts (6.1).

Table 6 **Is health a 'public good'?**

Q.A5 'If a real market in healthcare existed, this would not stop some of it being run by government because healthcare is a natural public good.'

	1	2	3	4	5	6	7	8	9	10	Avg.
Newspaper health journalists	0	1	1	1	1	0	3	1	0	2	6.3
Electronic media health journalists	1	0	0	0	2	1	0	1	2	3	7.3
Health and social policy academics	5	1	1	0	1	0	1	1	0	0	3.0
Party political health spokesmen	2	3	0	1	1	1	1	1	0	0	3.8
Members of the H of C HSC	0	1	0	1	0	1	2	0	4	1	7.2
Party political advisers	1	1	2	1	2	1	1	0	0	1	4.6
Senior civil servants	4	0	0	1	0	1	1	0	2	1	4.9
Health interest group representatives	0	0	2	1	0	1	3	2	0	1	6.3
Think tank policy experts	4	1	4	0	0	1	0	0	0	0	2.4
Senior medical and health professionals	2	0	0	0	3	0	2	3	0	0	5.5
Totals	19	8	10	6	10	7	14	9	8	9	
Overall average 5.1											

While members of think tanks might be in the business of challenging seemingly plausible assumptions, with regard to senior medical and health professionals it is possible that their neutrality stems from the fact that they see themselves as being much more relevant to the protection of people from contagious disease than government agencies or departments. In short, they see themselves as independent agents and advocates on the front line of healthcare delivery – regardless of whether healthcare in general is provided privately or by the state.

In response to the statement 'If a real market in healthcare existed, this would not stop some of it being run by government because healthcare is a natural public good' all respondent categories answered within the relatively wide (negative) 2.4 to (positive) 7.3 range. Overall, the opinion-forming 100 averaged a score of 5.1; see Table 6.

Again, there were important differences between categories. While electronic media health journalists (7.3) and newspaper health journalists (6.3) tended to agree with the statement that healthcare is a natural public good, there was clear disagreement from think tank policy experts (2.4) and health and social policy academics (3.0). Such strong rejections of the concept from these two latter respondent groups suggest that they either saw the question as being contentious or they view healthcare as being a natural private good. Of course, it is also possible that the non-academic categories do not understand the proper economic meaning of the term 'public good'.

In response to the statement 'Because people's healthcare is unpredictable some of its costs will always have to be covered by government – private arrangements such as insurance cannot do it all', all respondent categories answered within the relatively wide

Table 7 **Predictability of healthcare costs**

Q.A6 'Because people's healthcare is unpredictable some of its costs will always have to be covered by government – private arrangements such as insurance cannot do it all.'

	1	2	3	4	5	6	7	8	9	10	Avg.
Newspaper health journalists	0	1	0	1	0	0	4	1	1	2	7.1
Electronic media health journalists	0	0	0	1	1	0	1	2	2	3	8.0
Health and social policy academics	3	0	0	0	1	0	2	1	1	2	5.9
Party political health spokesmen	1	0	0	0	1	0	1	3	2	2	7.5
Members of the H of C HSC	0	0	0	1	0	0	0	3	1	5	8.7
Party political advisers	0	4	1	0	1	1	0	2	0	1	4.8
Senior civil servants	3	1	3	0	1	0	1	0	1	0	3.5
Health interest group representatives	0	0	0	1	1	1	2	1	1	3	7.6
Think tank policy experts	3	1	1	0	2	1	0	1	0	1	4.2
Senior medical and health professionals	1	0	3	0	0	0	2	4	0	0	5.6
Totals	11	7	8	4	8	3	13	18	9	19	

Overall average 6.2

(negative) 3.5 to (positive) 8.7 range. Overall, the opinion-forming 100 averaged a slightly positive score of 6.2 (see Table 7).

While members of the House of Commons Health Select Committee (8.7), electronic media health journalists (8.0) and newspaper health journalists (7.1) tended to agree with the statement, senior civil servants (3.5), the think tank policy experts (4.2) and party political advisers on health and social policy (4.8) all disagreed. Senior medical and health professionals (5.6) and the health and social policy academics (5.9) had a more or less neutral position.

In response to the statement 'If people are covered by private healthcare, there is a greater incentive for them to use it and get their money's worth' all respondent categories answered within the (slightly negative) 4.3 to (reasonably positive) 7.6 range. Overall, the opinion-forming 100 averaged a slightly positive score of 6.0 (Table 8).

Table 8 **Moral hazard**

Q.A7 *'If people are covered by private healthcare, there is a greater incentive for them to use it and get their money's worth.'*

	1	2	3	4	5	6	7	8	9	10	Avg.
Newspaper health journalists	0	0	1	0	3	0	2	3	1	0	6.5
Electronic media health journalists	0	1	0	1	0	0	1	3	2	2	7.5
Health and social policy academics	1	0	1	1	0	1	3	1	0	2	6.3
Party political health spokesmen	2	1	0	0	3	2	2	0	0	0	4.5
Members of the H of C HSC	0	0	0	1	0	0	4	2	2	1	7.6
Party political advisers	0	0	1	2	0	3	1	3	0	0	6.0
Senior civil servants	4	0	2	0	0	0	1	1	2	0	4.3
Health interest group representatives	0	1	1	2	4	0	1	0	0	1	5.0
Think tank policy experts	1	0	1	0	1	1	2	2	1	1	6.4
Senior medical and health professionals	0	0	0	3	1	0	1	2	3	0	6.7
Totals	8	3	7	10	12	7	18	17	11	7	

Overall average 6.0

While senior civil servants (4.3), party political spokesmen (4.5) and health interest group representatives (5.0) erred on the side of disagreement, members of the House of Commons Health Select Committee (7.6), electronic media journalists (7.5), senior medical and health professionals (6.7), newspaper health journalists (6.5) and think tank policy experts (6.4) tended to agree with the view that if people were covered by private healthcare they would have a greater incentive to use it.

There is further analysis of these findings in Chapter 7. It is clear, however, from just a cursory analysis of these responses that politicians and health interest groups are more sceptical of a market economy in health than academics, those working for think thanks and, interestingly, those advising political parties. The media also seems to show a high degree of scepticism of the market.

Opinions on 'government failure'

The questions in Section B – numbered 8–14 – again invited respondents to agree or disagree with particular statements. As with Section A (above), but this time dealing with 'Opinions towards government failure in healthcare', each respondent was given the following instruction: 'On a scale of 1–10, with 1 being "strongly disagree" and 10 being "strongly agree", can you please tell me what you think of the following statement?'

Table 9 **Problems of government monopoly**

Q.B8 'If a system of real state healthcare existed, a market providing people with choices would still have to be allowed to stop problems of monopoly.'

	1	2	3	4	5	6	7	8	9	10	Avg.
Newspaper health journalists	0	0	0	1	0	1	1	3	2	2	7.9
Electronic media health journalists	1	2	1	0	1	1	1	1	1	1	5.3
Health and social policy academics	0	0	1	0	1	1	1	0	1	5	8.0
Party political health spokesmen	2	0	1	0	1	0	1	3	0	2	6.1
Members of the H of C HSC	1	0	0	1	0	3	1	2	2	0	6.4
Party political advisers	1	0	0	0	1	0	1	2	2	3	7.7
Senior civil servants	0	0	0	1	0	1	2	1	1	4	8.1
Health interest group representatives	0	1	2	0	1	2	0	1	1	2	6.2
Think tank policy experts	1	0	0	0	0	0	1	2	2	4	8.2
Senior medical and health professionals	0	0	2	2	0	4	0	0	1	1	5.7
Totals	6	3	7	5	5	13	9	15	13	24	

Overall average 6.9

In response to the statement 'If a system of real state healthcare existed, a market providing people with choices would still have to be allowed to stop problems of monopoly' all respondent categories answered within the (neutral) 5.3 to (positive) 8.2 range. Overall, the opinion-forming 100 averaged a reasonably positive score of 6.9 (see Table 9).

Nevertheless, below this headline average there were some important differences. While think tank policy experts (8.2), senior civil servants (8.1), health and social policy academics (8.0), newspaper health journalists (7.9) and party political advisers on health and social policy (7.7) tended to agree with the view expressed, health interest group representatives (6.2), party political health spokesmen (6.1), senior medical and health professionals (5.7) and electronic media health journalists (5.3) were all respondent categories that were much more cautious in their answers – suggesting, perhaps, that they would not be discontented with a state healthcare system that prohibited private provision.

Significantly, no respondent category overtly disagreed with the statement and therefore with the idea that, under a real state healthcare system, a market providing people with choices would still have to exist if problems of monopoly were to be ameliorated.

Table 10 **Consumer ignorance in state healthcare systems**

Q.B9 'If a system of real state healthcare existed, people would have to be allowed to access a wide range of competing health information so that individuals could overcome the problems of consumer ignorance.'

	1	2	3	4	5	6	7	8	9	10	Avg.
Newspaper health journalists	0	0	0	2	1	0	0	0	1	6	8.2
Electronic media health journalists	0	0	0	0	2	0	1	1	3	3	8.2
Health and social policy academics	0	0	0	0	1	0	2	1	1	5	8.6
Party political health spokesmen	0	0	1	0	1	0	1	2	4	1	7.7
Members of the H of C HSC	0	0	0	0	0	1	3	4	1	1	7.8
Party political advisers	0	0	0	0	0	1	3	1	2	3	8.3
Senior civil servants	0	0	0	0	0	0	1	3	1	5	9.0
Health interest group representatives	0	0	1	0	0	1	2	2	2	2	7.7
Think tank policy experts	0	0	0	0	1	0	2	1	3	3	8.4
Senior medical and health professionals	0	0	0	0	0	2	2	3	2	1	7.8
Totals	0	0	2	2	6	5	17	18	20	30	

Overall average 8.1

In response to the statement 'If a system of real state health-care existed, people would have to be allowed to access a wide range of competing health information so that individuals could overcome the problems of consumer ignorance' all respondent categories answered within a remarkably narrow, consensual and positive 7.7 to 9.0 range. Overall, as shown in Table 10, the opinion-forming 100 averaged a positive score of 8.1.

With all respondent categories generally agreeing with the idea that under state healthcare people would still require competing channels of health information to overcome the problems of consumer ignorance, it was clear that the respond-ents were sensitive to the limits and unintended consequences of state power. As if inherently accepting of the subjectivity of knowledge and the medical discovery process, all categories seemingly accepted that a legal or black market in information

Table 11 **The role of charities in a state healthcare system**

Q.B10 'If a system of real state healthcare existed, there would still be a need for many private healthcare charities and groups to protect the poor and chronically sick from neglect.'

	1	2	3	4	5	6	7	8	9	10	Avg.
Newspaper health journalists	1	0	0	1	2	1	1	2	1	1	6.3
Electronic media health journalists	1	1	0	1	1	0	1	2	1	2	6.4
Health and social policy academics	0	1	1	0	0	1	2	1	0	4	7.3
Party political health spokesmen	0	1	2	0	0	0	2	2	2	1	6.6
Members of the H of C HSC	0	1	0	0	0	0	0	2	4	3	8.4
Party political advisers	0	0	3	1	0	0	4	1	0	1	5.9
Senior civil servants	1	0	4	0	0	1	0	1	0	3	5.7
Health interest group representatives	0	0	1	1	0	1	1	2	1	3	7.5
Think tank policy experts	1	0	0	0	1	1	0	3	0	4	7.6
Senior medical and health professionals	0	3	2	0	0	0	1	2	1	1	5.4
Totals	4	7	13	4	4	5	12	18	10	23	
Overall average 6.7											

would exist and help overcome the problems of consumer ignorance. Significantly, no respondent category believed that a real
state healthcare system could on its own overcome the problems
of consumer ignorance.

In response to the statement 'If a system of real state healthcare existed, there would still be a need for many private healthcare charities and groups to protect the poor and chronically sick
from neglect' all respondent categories answered within a relatively narrow (neutral) 5.4 to (very positive) 8.4 range. Overall, the
opinion-forming 100 averaged a slightly positive score of 6.7 (see
Table 11).

While members of the House of Commons Health Select
Committee (8.4), think tank policy experts (7.6), health interest
group representatives (7.5) and health and social policy academics
(7.3) all agreed with the inevitability of private healthcare charities and groups playing a vital role in protecting the poor and
chronically sick from neglect (even under a system of real state
healthcare), senior medical and health professionals (5.4), senior
civil servants (5.7) and party political advisers on health and social
policy (5.9) were less sure. For the latter three respondent categories such a view is more controversial.

Having said that, no respondent category overtly disagreed
with the idea that under any state system private healthcare charities and groups will always have an important role to play for the
poor and chronically sick, thus accepting what seems clear from 50
years of experience – that the welfare state cannot deal completely
with people's most personal needs.

Table 12 **The role of the private sector and contagious disease**

Q.B11 'If a system of real state healthcare existed, private healthcare would still have to intervene to help protect people from such external factors as contagious disease.'

	1	2	3	4	5	6	7	8	9	10	Avg.
Newspaper health journalists	3	2	1	0	1	1	1	1	0	0	3.6
Electronic media health journalists	2	4	3	1	0	0	0	0	0	0	2.3
Health and social policy academics	2	2	0	1	2	0	2	0	0	1	4.4
Party political health spokesmen	3	1	0	1	2	1	1	0	1	0	4.1
Members of the H of C HSC	1	1	1	1	1	2	0	2	0	1	5.3
Party political advisers	2	1	5	1	0	1	0	0	0	0	2.9
Senior civil servants	4	0	3	0	1	0	1	0	0	1	3.5
Health interest group representatives	1	2	0	1	1	1	1	3	0	0	5.1
Think tank policy experts	1	1	0	0	2	1	0	2	1	2	6.5
Senior medical and health professionals	0	4	2	1	1	0	0	1	0	1	4.1
Totals	19	18	15	7	11	7	6	9	2	6	

Overall average 4.1

In response to the statement 'If a system of real state healthcare existed, private healthcare would still have to intervene to help protect people from such external factors as contagious disease', all respondent categories answered within the relatively broad (very negative) 2.3 to (slightly positive) 6.5 range. Overall, the opinion-forming 100 averaged a negative score of 4.1. The results are summarised in Table 12.

While think tank policy experts (6.5) just erred on the side of the positive, all the other respondent categories tended towards a negative view. Electronic media health journalists (2.3), party political advisers on health and social policy (2.9) and newspaper health journalists (3.6) were all overt in their disagreement with the idea that private healthcare had much, if anything, to offer in terms of protection when it came to such external factors as contagious disease.

Significantly, no respondent category overtly supported the

idea that, under a system of real state healthcare, private healthcare would have much to offer against the societal threat of contagious disease. This would suggest that opinion formers tend to the view that a state healthcare system can, if nothing else, deal reasonably well with contagious disease.

Table 13 **Healthcare as a private good**

Q.B12 'If a system of real state healthcare existed, this would not stop some of it being run by a private market because healthcare is a natural private good.'

	1	2	3	4	5	6	7	8	9	10	Avg.
Newspaper health journalists	0	1	1	1	1	0	2	2	1	1	6.3
Electronic media health journalists	0	2	1	2	0	2	1	2	0	0	5.0
Health and social policy academics	1	0	0	1	1	1	2	1	0	3	6.8
Party political health spokesmen	0	1	1	0	1	1	2	1	3	0	6.5
Members of the H of C HSC	1	1	1	0	2	4	0	0	1	0	5.8
Party political advisers	1	0	1	0	3	0	1	3	1	0	5.9
Senior civil servants	0	0	1	0	1	0	0	4	1	3	7.9
Health interest group representatives	0	0	1	1	1	1	0	4	0	2	7.0
Think tank policy experts	0	1	0	0	2	1	1	1	1	3	7.2
Senior medical and health professionals	1	2	0	0	2	1	0	3	0	1	5.5
Totals	4	8	7	5	14	11	9	21	8	13	

Overall average 6.3

In response to the statement 'If a system of real state healthcare existed, this would not stop some of it being run by a private market because healthcare is a natural private good', all respondent categories answered within the relatively narrow (slightly negative) 5.0 to (positive) 7.9 range. Overall, the opinion-forming 100 averaged a slightly positive score of 6.3 (see Table 13).

While senior civil servants (7.9), think tank policy experts (7.2), health interest group representatives (7.0) and health and social policy academics (6.8) erred on the side of the positive, all the other respondent categories found the statement more controversial. Electronic media health journalists (5.0), senior medical and health professionals (5.5) and party political advisers on health and social policy (5.9) all provided more or less neutral scores.

Significantly, no respondent category overtly disagreed with the view that under a system of real state healthcare some of it would still be run by a private market because healthcare is a natural private good.

Table 14 Is there a necessity for private funds?

Q.B13 'Because people's healthcare is unpredictable some of its costs will always have to be covered by private healthcare – government arrangements such as taxation cannot do it all.'

	1	2	3	4	5	6	7	8	9	10	Avg.
Newspaper health journalists	0	1	0	0	1	4	0	1	1	2	6.8
Electronic media health journalists	2	1	2	1	2	0	0	1	1	0	4.1
Health and social policy academics	0	0	0	1	0	1	2	2	0	4	8.0
Party political health spokesmen	1	0	0	0	0	1	2	2	3	1	7.4
Members of the H of C HSC	0	0	3	1	0	0	2	1	1	2	6.4
Party political advisers	1	0	0	1	1	0	3	1	1	2	6.8
Senior civil servants	1	1	0	1	1	0	2	1	0	3	6.4
Health interest group representatives	0	1	1	0	0	3	2	2	0	1	6.3
Think tank policy experts	0	1	0	0	2	0	0	2	0	5	7.8
Senior medical and health professionals	0	2	1	1	0	0	2	2	1	1	6.0
Totals	5	7	7	6	7	9	15	15	8	21	
Overall average 6.5											

In response to the statement 'Because people's healthcare is unpredictable some of its costs will always have to be covered by private healthcare – government arrangements such as taxation cannot do it all', all respondent categories answered within the (slightly negative) 4.1 to (positive) 8.0 range. Overall, the opinion-forming 100 averaged a slightly positive score of 6.5.

While health and social policy academics (8.0), think tank

policy experts (7.8), party political advisers on health and social policy (6.8) and newspaper health journalists (6.8) were all positive, electronic media health journalists were negative (4.1). Senior civil servants (6.4), health interest group representatives (6.3) and senior medical and health professionals (6.0) provided more neutral responses.

Significantly, no respondent category profoundly disagreed with the view. There does not appear to be any strong affinity for the original vision that many had of the NHS providing all health-care needs without any charges or alternative private provision.

Table 15 **Abuse of state healthcare**

Q.B14 'If people are covered by state healthcare, there is a greater incentive for them to use it and get their money's worth.'

	1	2	3	4	5	6	7	8	9	10	Avg.
Newspaper health journalists	0	0	1	0	3	0	2	2	2	0	6.6
Electronic media health journalists	1	2	0	0	2	0	2	1	1	1	5.6
Health and social policy academics	0	0	1	1	1	0	2	0	0	5	7.6
Party political health spokesmen	0	1	2	0	1	1	2	2	1	0	5.8
Members of the H of C HSC	0	1	0	0	1	0	1	2	2	3	7.8
Party political advisers	0	1	0	0	2	1	3	1	1	1	6.6
Senior civil servants	0	0	1	1	3	0	1	1	1	2	6.6
Health interest group representatives	0	1	1	2	2	1	1	1	0	1	5.4
Think tank policy experts	0	0	0	0	1	1	2	2	2	2	7.9
Senior medical and health professionals	0	0	2	0	1	2	0	1	2	2	6.9
Totals	1	6	8	4	17	6	16	13	12	17	
Overall average 6.6											

In response to the statement 'If people are covered by state healthcare, there is a greater incentive for them to use it and get their money's worth' all respondent categories answered within a (neutral) 5.4 to (positive) 7.9 range. Overall, the opinion-forming 100 averaged a slightly positive score of 6.6. The results are shown in Table 15.

While think tank policy experts (7.9), health and social policy academics (7.6) and senior medical and health professionals (6.9) were all positive, health interest group representatives (5.4) and electronic media health journalists (5.6) provided middling scores.

Significantly, no respondent category profoundly disagreed with the view. It would seem that the problem of moral hazard is perceived as important within both state and private healthcare systems.

There was greater consensus among the different groups of respondents with regard to the questions in Section B. Nevertheless, two things are noteworthy. There is general acceptance of and welcome for private provision and finance even within a state-oriented system. Second, once again confidence in state-provided healthcare was greater among the political class than amongst academics.

Parameters in the healthcare debate

The questions in Section C – numbered 15–21 – sought more open-ended responses so as to further clarify the conceptual boundaries surrounding commonly held notions of health economics and therefore to expose some of the current healthcare debate's limitations and deficiencies.

Question C15 demanded an open response to the following statement: 'In healthcare, what would be the consequences of a genuine, private, market system?'

In reply, most of the newspaper health journalists expressed concern with the 'inequity' such a system would bring and they tended to focus on the consequences of a more open market in health information. Many saw limitations in such a system. These limitations were expressed in phrases such as 'there would be an underclass'; 'it would be inequitable/expensive'; 'there would be big holes in the cover'; 'it would marginalise some people but benefit lots of people/be potentially inequitable'; 'it could lead to a degree of exclusion for lower-income people'. Others, however, stressed the perceived benefits, making comments such as: 'private healthcare would lead to better standards/increased competition/increased access to information'; 'the well informed would do better'; 'eventual improvement to poor and chronically sick although possibly not in the transition period'. Here, the over-whelming majority tended to associate a genuine private market with 'greater cost' and more 'expense'. More and better informa-tion would disproportionately empower the better off.

Likewise, electronic media health journalists also tended to believe that such a system 'would leave society's more vulner-able with an inferior service'; 'more would be spent on a system that covered fewer people … those who could afford more would get better healthcare'. A genuine private market system 'would neglect the needy and chronic illness'; the 'very poor would be very poorly served'. As if a free market encourages a zero-sum game with a fixed quality of wealth, one respondent concluded, 'Doctors and nurses would go to better hospitals leading to a long-term disaster.' Another stated, 'Lack of access for less well off – better-funded system in the short term.'

Health and social policy academics were much more positive in their responses: 'better access to services and more innovation'; 'everyone in society would be better off … poor would get better treatment and care'; 'lower cost, diversity of approaches, fast medical progress'. One respondent concluded, 'there would be more expenditure overall but there would also be better health for the same expenditure'; another asserted: 'new medical techniques and funding mechanisms would be discovered that we currently cannot imagine'.

The responses from the party political health spokesmen were very mixed. While some saw 'greater diversity of provision', 'more incentive to improve', 'less waiting', 'greater choice' and 'people would have a [greater] interest in their own health', others asserted: 'could lead to problems for some', 'chronically sick [would be] uninsurable and dependent on charity', 'look at the USA to see private market horror'. While generally believing the market would be more 'efficient', most remained worried about the poor and long-term ill.

Most respondents from the House of Commons Health Select Committee tended to the negative. For them, a genuine private market would encourage the 'poor to go back to a dark Victorian age'; it would be 'too expensive' with 'little investment for the poor'. That said, there were also members who asserted that more involvement of the private sector would have benefits because 'private health is strong on quality', 'much better for everyone, state healthcare has not been good for the poor', and 'much better patient-focused service'. While one person interpreted the question in the immediate terms of the NHS, 'disaster for the health service', another stated 'quicker'.

The party political advisers on health and social policy, though, were strikingly positive. They saw a genuine private market health system as being 'cheaper, faster, better, more democratic'; 'lead[ing] to higher standards, [greater] innovation and higher efficiency … over time lower costs'; 'more efficient … and improved outcomes for the poor in all probability compared with the state system'; 'access would be quicker'; 'there would be more consumer power, better access, higher standards of responsiveness'; it would 'allow growth' and even 'address more need, allow a thousand blooms to flourish'. Indeed, in this group there were only three negative respondents, who suggested the problems of: 'rising drug prices', 'lack of universal coverage' and 'putting more pressure on health infrastructure'.

For senior civil servants the picture was mixed. Some were clearly worried by the notion of a genuine market and what it might mean: 'poorer and more deprived communities would suffer unless there were safeguards'; 'government would have to regulate to ensure fairness' and '[would require] government as purchaser especially with regard to chronic disease' were all common responses. Others welcomed a market approach, asserting: 'increased accessibility, drive up quality'; 'appropriate use of resources, better-informed consumer decisions'; 'better outcomes for consumers'; and 'better innovation, better healthcare at lower cost'.

Health interest group representatives gave, as one might expect, a wide-ranging and varied set of responses. While some were concerned with the issues of inequality and poverty, others saw a market as providing a framework for more choice, better quality and greater efficiency. Some suggested that people are not capable of being consumers and that costs would be high.

Alongside the party political advisers on health and social policy (above), the think tank policy experts tended to see a genuine private market in positive terms. For them, such a system would deliver: 'much easier access ... [and] more new practices [such as] mobile operating theatres'. It would also offer 'higher standards for all', and they pointed out that universal access is not achieved at present. One respondent suggested that there would be 'vast, vast, vast improvement, service up, prices down, [as with] cosmetic surgery there would be a true market with lots of competition'. Few made negative comments, although a couple of respondents did assert: 'But you need a mix', 'many people uncovered could not afford insurance, [here, the] state would have to intervene'.

The final group, the senior medical and health professionals, tended to be negative about a genuine market system. They particularly cited perceived inequalities with the poor being disadvantaged. The few positive comments included: 'competition could only be good', 'people would take better care of themselves … more innovation', and 'more choice'.

Question C16 asked: 'In healthcare, what would be the consequences of a genuine, full-blown, state system?'

As with C15, many of the newspaper health journalists expressed an interest in 'information', citing 'reduced access to information' as a problem with full-blown state healthcare. Overall, the journalists were damning of a genuine, full-blown state system, with concerns being expressed about limited choice, lack of innovation, corruption, slowness to introduce new treatments, insensitivity to patient choice and demand, waiting lists, rationing, reduced research and development and inefficient distribution. On the positive side, some of the responses were self-consciously utopian, one suggesting that, in an ideal world, 'good, well-costed health provision would be available for all but with less choice and freedom.'

The electronic media health journalists tended to believe that such a system 'would be very expensive and inefficient' and that 'taxation would go up and up'. They also believed it would be 'bureaucratic and slow moving'. While one respondent commented 'the NHS is pretty close to this already' another commented that there would be 'long-term decline in service and delivery as there [is] no private sector benchmark. With no pressure on doctors and hospitals to treat people as customers [we] will be stuck in the 1970s'. Here only one respondent was positive: 'if affordable, ideal. If a good state system evolved needs would be met'.

The health and social policy academics were damning in their responses to suggestions of a completely state-run system: 'short-ages, crisis over rationing, people who would go abroad to exercise choice', 'inconsistency between expectations and availability', 'everyone worse off. Poorest and most inarticulate would die [as in] Soviet Russia and North Korea. No innovation', 'poor quality, less choice' were representative responses. Significantly, some respondents in this group questioned the medical monopoly that currently underpins all systems of healthcare and even the impact that a full-blown state healthcare system would have on healthcare workers: 'unless the problem of medical professional monopoly is dealt with it would be as inefficient as it is today'.

While responses from the party political health spokesmen were mixed, many highlighted their concerns with rationing queues and rationing. It was suggested that, without rationing, costs would be uncontrollable. Eighty per cent of respondents in this group complained about rationing, high costs and the perceived inevitability of queuing.

Although with C15 (above) many respondents from the House of Commons Health Select Committee appeared to be opposed to a genuine private market in health, when asked to comment on a full-blown state system they were equally scathing. In this group only one person was overtly supportive, suggesting that there could be 'decent healthcare for everyone irrespective of their background, birth and status in life, good healthcare for all is the ideal, it is possible'.

The party political advisers on health and social policy were strikingly negative as regards a full-blown state system. They foresaw higher costs and middle-class capture combined with less accountability, a black market and inefficiency. The positive comments were: 'you need state and private in competition to make a good system' and 'greater universal access'.

For senior civil servants the picture would be universally worse with low dynamic efficiency in the medium-to-long term being a suggested outcome, together with a risk of no innovation and poor quality. Representatives of health interest groups, however, gave a varied set of responses. On the negative side they suggested that there would be an arrogant monopoly provider and patients would have little incentive to seek knowledge or information about health and healthcare. It was also suggested that a full-blown system would be a 'heavy burden on the taxpayer'. Other comments included: 'monopolistic, unresponsive services', 'lack of access to information, quality levels at a minimum, rising costs', 'failure, failing standards, system scuppered by demand, low capital investment'. On the positive side, however, it was commented that 'there would be universal coverage, higher standards throughout the service, a higher amount of GDP would go to healthcare and no waiting lists', and 'everyone would achieve equitable treatment in quality and speed if paid for by taxation'.

The think tank policy experts tended to see a genuine full-blown state healthcare system in negative terms. For them, such a system would deliver: 'rationing by queuing, failing standards, monopoly', 'lowering of standards', 'no incentives to improve', 'poor cost control, inequitable access, no universal coverage'.

From the senior medical and health professionals the responses were mixed. Welcoming the statement, respondents said 'it should be an improvement on present', 'should give equal access and quality based on demand, if adequately resourced', 'if it worked … people would get appropriate care'. On the negative side it was suggested that: doctors would become lazy and politicians become gods; that not enough money could be provided by taxation to have a full-blown state system; and there would be a lack of choice and very high costs.

Question C17 was designed to pit a private system against a market system. The results are shown in Table 16.

Table 16 **State and private monopolies in healthcare**

Q.C17 'In healthcare, which is more prone to the problems of monopoly?'

	The state	*The market*
Newspaper health journalists	10	00
Electronic media health journalists	06	04
Health and social policy academics	09	01
Party political health spokesmen	10	00
Members of the H of C HSC	07	03
Party political advisers	08	02
Senior civil servants	10	00
Health interest group representatives	08	02
Think tank policy experts	10	00
Senior medical and health professionals	04	06
Totals	**82**	**18**

An overwhelming 82 per cent said the state was more prone to monopoly. Moreover, all respondent categories chose the state except for senior medical and health professionals. One hundred per cent of think tank policy experts, newspaper health journalists, party political health spokesmen and civil servants chose the state, as did 90 per cent of health and social policy academics, 80 per cent of health interest group representatives and 80 per cent of party political advisers on health and social policy.

Question C18 asked: 'In healthcare, which two of the following four groups has most to gain from statutory restrictions on the advertising of medicines: medical professionals, private health bosses, Treasury ministers, consumers?'

Table 17 **Gainers from restrictions on advertising**

Q.C18 'In healthcare, which two of the following four groups has most to gain from statutory restrictions on the advertising of medicines?'

	Medical professionals	Private health bosses	Treasury ministers	Consumers
Newspaper health journalists	05	02	10	03
Electronic media health journalists	08	01	06	05
Health and social policy academics	08	04	07	01
Party political health spokesmen	05	03	09	03
MPs on H of C Health Select Committee	03	04	09	04
Party political advisers on health/soc. policy	06	04	10	00
Senior civil servants	07	02	07	04
Health interest group representatives	06	04	05	05
Think tank policy experts	09	00	10	01
Senior medical and health professionals	04	05	08	03
Totals	**61**	**29**	**81**	**29**

In response (see Table 17), an overwhelming majority (81 per cent) chose Treasury ministers and a considerable majority (61 per cent) chose medical professionals. The other two groups – private health bosses and consumers – tied, with both receiving 29 per cent.

These headline numbers are important because they suggest that the respondents overwhelmingly see the statutory restrictions on medicines as primarily benefiting cost-containing politicians. Likewise a majority (61 per cent) see such restrictions as enhancing the professional power of the medical interest groups. Significantly, while 90 per cent of think tank policy experts view medical professionals as being key beneficiaries of statutory restrictions on the advertising of medicines, 100 per cent see Treasury ministers in this light too.

Question C19 asked about the efficacy of the public and private sectors in relation to contagious diseases – the results are shown in Table 18.

Table 18 **Politicians and contagious disease**

Q.C19 'Which one of the following statements would you choose to best describe your attitude? (A) If a contagious disease threatens Britain, I would trust politicians and government to be open from the start and to do the right things. (B) If a contagious disease threatens Britain, I do not believe politicians and government would be open from the start and to do the right things.'

	Attitude A	*Attitude B*
Newspaper health journalists	01	09
Electronic media health journalists	03	07
Health and social policy academics	03	07
Party political health spokesmen	08	02
Members of the H of C Health Select Committee	04	06
Party political advisers on health and social policy	05	05
Senior civil servants	05	05
Health interest group representatives	02	08
Think tank policy experts	02	08
Senior medical and health professionals	01	09
Totals	**34**	**66**

In response, a substantial 66 per cent chose option B and thereby expressed the view that if a contagious disease threatened

Britain they would not trust politicians and government to be open from the start and to do the right things. Only a third of all respondents – 34 per cent – expressed the view that they would trust politicians and the government. Significantly, 90 per cent of newspaper health journalists, 90 per cent of senior medical and health professionals, 80 per cent of think tank policy experts and 80 per cent of health interest group representatives all chose option B. Only a majority of party political health spokesmen – 80 per cent – had confidence that politicians and government would be open from the start and do the right things. Both party political advisers on health and social policy and senior civil servants were divided with 50 per cent choosing A and 50 per cent choosing B.

Invited to give open-ended comment on the reasons for their answer, one newspaper health journalist commented that he was 'not completely cynical'; he believed in 'cock-up rather than conspiracy'. Across all respondent categories trust of politicians and government was low. While some believed that by the nature of their work there would always be unintended consequences for politicians, a clear majority believed that government could not be trusted.

While some believed that often it is not always right for ministers to be open from the start of an outbreak – 'wouldn't be open but that might be the right thing to do, especially in [an] epidemic', 'openness and doing the right thing can be competing' – just over a third were positive: 'the Department of Health and the government machine are good with plans for this kind of crisis', 'you can trust politicians and government but they won't necessarily get it all right', 'they do their best, systems are in place for this', 'the health and other ministries would do their best – of any party. They have good planning, expertise and people. They would do the correct thing'.

Question C20 asked: 'Many people argue that because disease and epidemics can impact on everyone in society, politicians must be in charge of public health. What do you think?'

In reply, most newspaper health journalists implicitly accepted that politicians should be in charge of public health: 'agree, regulatory role', 'would have to be in a democratically elected society', 'public health is a legitimate government issue', 'someone must be in charge, politicians are elected', 'agree but not solely, could just coordinate', 'legitimate coordination role', 'need some sort of regulating role', 'this is where public health meets defence'. Only three people took a fundamentally different view, suggesting that: the government should not necessarily be involved, that 'providers could be private' and, in one case, 'no, strongly disagree, would not trust politicians with total authority, small role in coordination and dissemination of information'.

Among the electronic media health journalists there was more general scepticism about the role of politicians in public health. Responses included: 'don't agree at all', 'if you look at the government's approach to BSE and foot and mouth political and financial considerations get in the way of the best solutions', 'not true, individuals are more educated than politicians think they are, individuals would make better choices than politicians'. Alternatively, some did see a role for politicians and government in this area: 'agree, government is about making stable, successful, happy societies – something as basic as healthcare is a government duty', 'there has to be a central overview of public health … politicians will always be involved in public health because of the way it is funded'.

Health and social policy academics again had mixed views.

Supporting this role for politicians, respondents made comments such as: 'broadly agree', 'yes, in large measure a national response is needed as public health in the nineteenth century showed'. One respondent commented: 'genuine emergencies need emergency action. Otherwise politicians should have a very limited role in public health. For example, the Black Death is like going to war so you would not use peacetime measures. However, this rarely happens, so government should keep out of public health'. Against the politicians, respondents asserted: 'in an ideal world a more disinterested body would be in charge', 'not necessarily politicians', 'disagree, don't think that just because something has universal effects it needs government action'. One respondent concluded: 'public health is increasingly the rubric used by Western political elites to justify the therapeutic state and a wide range of health fascist restrictions and bans on people's freedom and lifestyle choice. Healthcare is a natural private good. Public health in its statist sense is an abomination'.

Party political health spokesmen were universally supportive of the idea of state involvement in public health. Not being able to perceive a market alternative, one respondent concluded: 'yes, an unelected alternative is not good.' While some members of the House of Commons Health Select Committee supported the role of politicians – 'common sense', 'yes of course, not a question' – others added the caveat that such work should be led by clinicians: 'No, independent public health doctors should be in charge', 'no, doctors, politicians must oversee the funding of a public health system [as] they are elected'. Interestingly, one person commented: 'yes, but there is too much nannying', while another concluded: '[there should be] private delivery of [an] active strategy of public health'.

Party political advisers on health and social policy displayed a wide range of opinion. Comments included: 'politicians should have an important role but this should not amount to a monopoly', 'patient groups should also have a role irrespective of government', 'a role for politicians in public health is easier to defend than in other areas of healthcare', 'ultimately agree, public health equals public good', 'don't agree at all, too simplistic, epidemics are usually regional not global', 'national politicians get it wrong, management should be at regional and global levels – public and private too'.

Overall, 60 per cent of senior civil servants generally agreed, commenting: 'do need to have public health responsibilities, but the government could be in charge of strategy', 'it should not be left to the private sector', 'you could argue that the state should concentrate on this and leave other healthcare alone'. The other respondents in this category put forward alternative views: 'no need to fund or provide', 'not true', 'not a must, other alternatives available'.

Health interest group representatives were mixed in their responses. Dividing up the various aspects of public health, one respondent concluded: 'charities and individuals have a role in keeping people healthy; however, there is a need for some sort of central coordinating body'. Significantly, most think tank policy experts disagreed with the statement in C20, a typical comment being: 'no, epidemics are rare things and the government track record in public health is not good'. On the other side a couple of respondents said: 'there is a political role for coordinating, but private bodies are better at dealing with outbreaks'.

Finally, senior medical and health professionals tended to see a role for politicians and government but were generally concerned with regulatory issues and the involvement of clinicians: 'doctors must be in charge, totally independent from government', 'ought to be given to public health experts and not politicised', 'the government need to be there but not necessarily politicians', 'not sure it has to be politicians, some sort of regulatory body', 'a disastrous idea', 'should not be run by politicians and should not be party dependent', 'delivery no, need healthcare professionals and a national framework'.

Question C21 asked: 'How do you react to the following statement? "The reason the poor and chronically sick are always neglected is because ever since Roman times, political elites in Britain have always sought to plan, control and regulate the provision of health services. Through the Roman military, then the Church, the Royal Colleges, Parliament, and the timeless granting of legislative favour, the state has always sought to empire-build and to control people's access to healthcare and medicine."'

In reply, most newspaper health journalists agreed with the statement but added various caveats: 'I am not quite so cynical, but element of truth', 'some truth … state systems do serve the middle classes better', 'probably do agree historically', 'sympathetic but would not knee-jerk agree', 'exaggeration', 'strongly agree, anecdotal evidence and record of government over the years shows this to be true however well intended'.

Conversely, most electronic media health journalists disagreed: 'don't agree at all, they are neglected not because of control but due to education, environment and social conditions', 'don't agree', 'this credits the state and politicians with far too much ability to control populations, I believe in cock-up rather than conspiracy, the state has been unable to care for the poor and chronically sick but not by design', 'disagree, various politicians attempted to expand healthcare beyond the elite', 'don't know, parts may be true', 'I don't believe they are always neglected'. A couple of respondents agreed with the statement in C20: 'the powers that be have always sought to influence healthcare as it affects people who vote for them, politicians have a more under-hand influence than people understand', 'parts may be true, poor get a worse deal by default, they are not articulate, cannot complain and their services are therefore not improved'.

The health and social policy academics surveyed offered varying – yet often more in-depth – responses: 'big historical generalisation ... generally the state does not have the capacity, especially control over the Church', 'while not claiming that the state is always motivated to maximise social welfare, reliance, mainly on private institutions (as in the USA), tends to exclude the poor even more strongly ... this is not an attack on private delivery of healthcare but on reliance mainly on private finance', 'don't agree fully with this historical analogy, the medieval period was a great mixture of provision and the types of medicine ... need to look at much wider social factors', 'to an extent true, money and power gets the foot in the door to health'. In addition to supportive responses such as 'agree' and 'agree with that', one respondent concluded: 'this statement is totally true because it focuses on the central question of power in society. From tribes in pre-history to the modern world, the chiefs and monarchs of the state have always granted monopolistic and legislative favour to the would-be monopolists of the day. Throughout the ages medical professionals, through the Church and then Parliament, have always sought state power and sold it in the name of the public good. As such, there has never been a necessary divorce between healthcare and political power. Throughout history, there has never been a genuine market in health provision. As such, the poor and chronically sick – the socially powerless – have always suffered. They have been marginalised and suffered at the hands of the public good'.

Similarly, the party political health spokesmen had firm views ranging from: 'something in that, inclined to agree' to 'completely over the top' and 'nonsense, far more complicated'. One Member of Parliament concluded: 'not characterised by state control. [The problem is a] lack of health provision overall. People were developing private arrangements before the NHS. Poor people have no market power, so they are left with a state system and are grateful for what they get … Not sure about the Church … since the advent of the welfare state, the inevitable price of state intervention is state control'.

Members of the House of Commons Health Select Committee tended to either hesitantly support the statement in C20 or steer a cautious middling path: 'not sure', 'not sure government has always been so involved', 'this is muddling the state with the churches and the colleges', 'sounds good', 'sounds too simplistic but interesting', 'there is always an issue of elite control, but elites can help the poor too', 'healthcare demands government acting for us all', 'elites have always oppressed the poor, but this is the fault of classes and power not the state'.

Party political advisers on health and social policy tended to express positive support with comments such as: 'agree', 'elements are true, but too universal', 'agree strongly', 'some elements of truth, but not universally true in twentieth century', 'very interesting, broadly agree, people and elites pursue their own power'. Only one person strongly disagreed: 'completely disagree. Politicians have created universal and free system that has given the poor the first ever access to healthcare. Healthcare can be provided by the private sector, but only to assist the state sector'.

Most senior civil servants surveyed tended to agree, commenting: 'partly true', 'yes', 'agree', 'states try to control costs', 'pretty cool'. Nevertheless, others were more critical: 'do not agree', 'don't really agree, don't think [the state] is anti-poor', 'strongly disagree, political intervention aims at equality of access, their failure is neither here nor there'.

The health interest group representatives were split down the middle. Some commented: 'elements of truth', 'couldn't disagree', 'probably partly true', 'agree', 'the reason for neglect of poor and sick is because the state has not learnt from private sector marketing'. On the other side of the argument, however, others said: 'disagree, despite criticism the state has not sought to empire-build or neglect, the state model is more likely to protect the poor', 'this is silly, there is an argument that the state is not good at healthcare provision but the NHS removed fear and dread of the poor for doctors and medical bills; healthcare is a human right, not a whim of the market or largesse of the rich'. Interestingly one respondent concluded: 'absolutely agreed up to the first Labour government, now defiantly not since the introduction of the NHS'.

A clear majority – 80 per cent – of the think tank policy experts surveyed strongly agreed: 'radical enthusiasm for this statement, problem has been worse since World War II', 'strongly agree', 'partly agree', 'quite true, but not whole truth', 'broadly agree', 'true, agree with spirit, interest groups do bend NHS to their own benefit', 'has to be true, nature of regulation; UK never had true alternative so therefore people are not fully trusting of the private sector'. Conversely, other respondents concluded: 'nonsense, tirade', 'I don't agree that the poor always miss out but there is unnecessary control in healthcare'.

Finally, senior medical and health professionals presented a wide range of responses: 'don't agree with the first part as the NHS spends loads on the poor', 'prefer to think that despite some politicisation of healthcare some people/politicians have genuinely wanted and attempted to improve healthcare of all', 'it is a cynical view that actually it is too expensive to provide adequate healthcare, but if government had enough money they would do it', 'access is controlled but not sure that this is why the poor and chronically sick are neglected, it is often a lack of education amongst the poor that leads to neglect rather than intention', 'agree', 'agree, this has evolved although this is not what was set out to be done', 'true, but not sure the state has sought to deliberately restrict access', 'sometimes the poor and chronically sick are helped by the state', 'don't agree that the poor always miss out but there is unnecessary control in healthcare', 'probably relevant at the time; the Church now has less impact but has been replaced by other interests over time'.

This chapter has simply reported the results of the survey. In Chapter 7, we analyse these responses further, in the context of different economic models of health provision.

7 BEYOND THE NHS: BOUNDARIES OF DISCOURSE ON BRITISH HEALTHCARE

Comparative analysis of responses of opinion formers on the merits of government and market provision

In this section we compare the answers to questions that looked at problems in the delivery of healthcare in the private and state sectors, comparing the responses to relevant questions firstly from Group A and, second, from Group B.

First, two statements examining the problem of monopoly were compared.

Q.A1 If a real market in healthcare existed, government would still have to intervene to stop problems of monopoly.

Average 5.9

Q.B8 If a system of real state healthcare existed, a market providing people with choices would still have to be allowed to stop problems of monopoly.

Average 6.9

Overall, the research found that while respondents were somewhat neutral towards the statement 'If a real market in healthcare existed, government would still have to intervene to stop problems of monopoly' (5.9), they tended to agree with the countervailing view (6.9) that: 'If a system of real state healthcare existed, a market providing people with choices would still have to be allowed to stop problems of monopoly'. Thus, respondents had greater anxieties about problems of monopoly in state than in private healthcare systems. Furthermore, there was a real sense that some kind of market and choice mechanism is an inevitable and necessary precondition for any viable healthcare system.

Whether this erring on the side of the laissez-faire market is the result of the current debate on the NHS or a broader scepticism about the theoretical limitations of state healthcare, however, remains unclear. What is clear is that when it comes to the notion of monopoly in state and market-driven healthcare systems the market currently tends to be seen as being less problematic. The market is perhaps seen in terms of being a better check on monopoly power than the state.

Information is often regarded as a problem in both private health markets and government-provided health services. Views on informational problems in both sectors were compared using the following pair of statements.

Q.A2 If a real market in healthcare existed, government would still have to intervene to provide objective information to overcome problems of consumer ignorance.

Average 5.8

Q.B9 If a system of real state healthcare existed, people would have to be allowed to access a wide range of competing health information so that individuals could overcome the problems of consumer ignorance.

Average 8.1

Likewise, the research found that while respondents were somewhat neutral towards the statement 'If a real market in healthcare existed, government would still have to intervene to provide objective information to overcome problems of consumer ignorance' (5.8), they strongly supported the countervailing view (8.1) that: 'If a system of real state healthcare existed, people would have to be allowed to access a wide range of competing health information so that individuals could overcome the problems of consumer ignorance'.

This is an important result. Asymmetric information is often seen as one of the problems of a market in health. It would appear that this notion was accepted and that it was also accepted, though not strongly, that government should intervene to deal with it. Information problems were, however, seen as more prevalent in the state than in the private sector. With most respondents questioning the benefits and even perhaps the notion of objective government information for healthcare consumers, the research found that under a system of real state healthcare (however conceived) a market providing people with access to a wide range of competing health information would still have to exist so that people could overcome the problems of consumer ignorance.

As such, there is a sense that some kind of market in health information is inevitable and/or desirable. Choice is seen as a means by which individuals can overcome the problems of informational consumer ignorance.

Next, we examine views on the ability of the public and private sectors to deal with the poor and chronically sick.

Q.A3 If a real market in healthcare existed, government would still have to intervene to protect the poor and chronically sick from neglect.

Average 7.3

Q.B10 If a system of real state healthcare existed, there would still be a need for many private healthcare charities and groups to protect the poor and chronically sick from neglect.

Average 6.7

The research found that while respondents were somewhat supportive of the view that 'if a system of real state healthcare existed, there would still be a need for many private healthcare charities and groups to protect the poor and chronically sick from neglect' (6.7), they were even more supportive of the equivalent statement related to the market provision of healthcare. Significantly, when seeking to protect the poor and chronically sick from neglect, respondents seemed to accept both a role for private healthcare institutions under state healthcare and a role for some form of government intervention under a market system.

Overall, respondents tended to see both systems as containing checks and balances on the other. Nevertheless, perhaps chiming with the rhetoric and agenda of public–private partnerships, and in contrast to the outlook when the NHS was first set up, the opinion formers surveyed no longer hold the view that the state should or could attempt to 'do it all'.

The stereotypical view of the 1940s that the NHS would provide all healthcare for everyone is no longer seen as appropriate – or even possible. When it comes to the poor and chronically sick, there is a general acceptance of a role both for private and state healthcare.

The problem of contagious diseases is often thought to lead to public-good characteristics in healthcare provision, and this was probed in reactions to the following pair of statements.

Q.A4 If a real market in healthcare existed, government would still have to intervene to help protect people from such external factors as contagious disease.

Average 7.6

Q.B11 If a system of real state healthcare existed, private healthcare would still have to intervene to help protect people from such external factors as contagious disease.

Average 4.1

The research found that while respondents were somewhat sceptical of the statement regarding the need to involve the private sector in the containment of contagious disease if a system of state healthcare existed, they were much more supportive of the view that the government would need to step in if there were a market-based system. Most people clearly see this as an area that demands direct government coordination and intervention – presumably accepting the 'public-good' arguments of the neoclassical model.

The public-good argument was then probed further in asking:

Q.A5 If a real market in healthcare existed, this would not stop some of it being run by government because healthcare is a natural public good.

Average 5.1

Q.B12 If a system of real state healthcare existed, this would not stop some of it being run by a private market because healthcare is a natural private good.

Average 6.3

Overall, the research found that respondents were neutral towards the statement 'If a real market in healthcare existed, this would not stop some of it being run by government because healthcare is a natural public good' and cautiously supported the view that healthcare is a natural private good. The consensus generally accepts that healthcare has both private- and public-good characteristics, and the respondents tended to see both systems as containing checks and balances on the other. Again this chimes with the contemporary rhetoric and agenda of public–private partnerships in healthcare. Opinion formers no longer hold the view, prevalent in the late 1940s, that the state could or should provide all healthcare for everyone. Indeed, both extremes were seen by the respondents as being problematic and as having profound limitations.

Problems with the predictability of health needs were then examined by asking for responses to the following:

Q.A6 Because people's healthcare is unpredictable some of its costs will always have to be covered by government – private arrangements such as insurance cannot do it all.

Average 6.2

Q.B13 Because people's healthcare is unpredictable some of its costs will always have to be covered by private healthcare – government arrangements such as taxation cannot do it all.

Average 6.6

Looking at the issue of insurance and taxation, the research found that while respondents were very marginally supportive of the need for government to cover some costs, because of unpredictability of need, it was also felt (slightly more strongly) that such unpredictability also militated against complete state finance of healthcare. Although the cleavage between the two groups was narrow at only 0.4, and both groups were only marginally positive with their scores, there is, again, a clear view emerging that government arrangements cannot provide everything. Whereas in the late 1940s one might have expected more respondents to have accepted the view that market-based systems based on insurance cannot 'do it all', today's opinion formers are slightly more sceptical of this historical and statist position.

This is not to say that the respondents are supportive of private medical insurance. Rather, the results suggest that there is a tentative acceptance of a role for private medical insurance alongside tax-funded healthcare.

The issue of moral hazard is perceived as important in any insurance-based system (private or government), and this was probed by asking for reactions to the following statements:

Q.A7 If people are covered by private healthcare, there is a greater incentive for them to use it and get their money's worth.

Average 6.0

Q.B14 If people are covered by state healthcare, there is a greater incentive for them to use it and 'get their money's worth'.

Average 6.6

Looking at the issue of private health and taxation, the research found that while respondents were marginally supportive of the view that moral hazard was a potential problem with private insurance, there was more support for the view that state provision created such moral hazard. Although the cleavage between the two groups was very narrow at only 0.6, and both groups were only marginally positive with their scores, there is again a clear pattern emerging. First, opinion formers seem to accept that moral hazard is possible. Second, they do not hold the utopian socialist view that people will behave in a solidaristic way when healthcare is financed by the state. The same assumption of economic rationality seems to prevail in the case of both the state and the private sector. Indeed, if anything, it seems to be assumed that the private sector will be more effective in controlling moral hazard.

Comparative analysis of views of opinion formers on government and market provision

Again, we look at views on the state and private sector, but this time analysing the open responses to pairs of questions about each sector.

Q.C15 In healthcare, what would be the consequences of a genuine, private, market system?

Q.C16 In healthcare, what would be the consequences of a genuine, full-blown, state system?

Concerning questions C15 and C16, it is interesting to note that many of the points made against a genuine, private, market in healthcare are also made against a genuine, full-blown, state system. Both are said to be: 'inequitable', 'two tier', 'rationed' and 'costly'.

Conversely, many of the positive points concerning a genuine private market system are also used to support a full-blown state system: 'efficient', 'poor would do better', 'more cost effective'.

While state healthcare was generally viewed as utopian, bureaucratic and requiring higher taxes, the market is generally differentiated in terms of encouraging innovation, better information and greater personal responsibility.

Overall, respondents tended to favour public–private partnerships – 'thank God we have always had a private health sector that can now be exploited' – and they also favoured regulation to 'ensure fairness'. Significantly, only one respondent questioned the monopoly that currently underpins all systems of healthcare: 'unless the problem of medical professional monopoly is dealt with [a genuine, private, market system would] be as inefficient as it is today'.

In response to the question 'In healthcare, which is more prone to the problems of monopoly?', 82 per cent answered 'the state' and 18 per cent 'the market'. Building on responses to A1 ('If a real market in healthcare existed, government would still have to intervene to stop problems of monopoly') and B8 ('If a system of real state healthcare existed, a market providing people with choices would still have to be allowed to stop problems of monopoly'), the response to C17 makes it clear that, under pressure, and with no opportunity for a graduated response, an overwhelming majority of respondents see the problems of monopoly power as being more associated with the state than the market.

This is interesting not least because it chimes with the position held by the advocates of the free-market Austrian school of economics that true monopolies only exist owing to state intervention. In the words of the Ludwig von Mises Institute:

> Economists of the classical school were right to define a
> monopoly as a government-grant privilege, for gaining legal
> rights to be a preferred producer is the only way to maintain
> a monopoly in a market setting. … A market society needs
> no antitrust policy at all; indeed, the state is the very source
> of the remaining monopolies we see in education, law,
> courts, and other areas.[1]

Although views on this question were not probed more
deeply, many of the monopolies that are likely to exist if markets
in healthcare provision were liberalised would be buttressed by
government regulation of professions and pharmaceuticals. It
is not possible to say whether the respondents to the monopoly
question regarded a fully private market as one that would be free
of regulation in these respects or not.

Question C18 examined one aspect of the regulation of
pharmaceuticals.

Q.C18 In healthcare, which two of the following four
groups has most to gain from statutory restrictions on the
advertising of medicines?

	Medical professionals	Private health bosses	Treasury ministers	Consumers
Totals	61	29	81	29

Importantly, an overwhelming majority of respondents –
81 per cent – saw Treasury ministers as having the most to gain
from the statutory restrictions on the advertising of medicines. In
other words, it was felt that restrictions on advertising were used
to promote consumer ignorance to artificially reduce the demand

---

1   See more on the Austrian Economics Forum at: http://austrianforum.com/
    index.php?showtopic=419.

for drugs. Again, a majority – 61 per cent – also identified medical professionals as generally benefiting from such restrictions.

Respondents also seem suspicious of the medical profession and its desire to control and censor. Only a minority of respondents – 29 per cent – believe that there would be any benefit for private healthcare bosses or consumers in having restricted access to the advertising of medicines. As such, the opinion formers surveyed seem to believe that government is rationing healthcare supply and information and that to preserve their own power and status doctors are complicit in this venture.

Question C19 related to contagious diseases. As stated in the previous chapter, in response to: If a contagious disease threatened Britain, would respondents trust – or not trust – 'politicians and government to be open from the start and to do the right things', a substantial 66 per cent expressed a negative view. Only a third of respondents – 34 per cent – expressed a positive view.

While most people who chose to comment tended to distrust politicians (and were highly critical of a perceived culture of spin and untruthfulness), respondents were most concerned with the unintended consequences of political action. They did not feel that the inadequacy of government response was a result of deliberate policy. Importantly, a number of people pointed out that openness was not always consonant with 'doing the right thing'.

Turning to the issue of externalities and public-good aspects of health provision, question C20 asked: 'Many people argue that because disease and epidemics can impact on everyone in society, politicians must be in charge of public health. What do you think?' In response, while a majority of respondents accepted that politicians should be in charge of public health, many added the caveat that they should involve other experts such as clinicians.

At the extreme, several respondents likened a contagious disease outbreak to a war: 'this is where public health meets defence'.

Alternatively, a small number of respondents focused on a broader definition of public health and attacked politicians' interventions in people's lifestyle choices. For example, one respondent said: 'public health is increasingly the rubric used by Western political elites to justify the therapeutic state and a wide range of health fascist restrictions and bans on people's freedom and lifestyle choice. Healthcare is a natural private good. Public health in its statist sense is an abomination'. Only a small minority, though, said that politicians and the state should have no role in public health.

In response to the statement: 'The reason the poor and chronically sick are always neglected is because ever since Roman times, political elites in Britain have always sought to plan, control and regulate the provision of health services. Through the Roman military, then the Church, the Royal Colleges, Parliament, and the timeless granting of legislative favour, the state has always sought to empire-build and to control people's access to healthcare and medicine', the 100 opinion formers surveyed were divided. While a number questioned the history presented – particularly as regards the medieval period – some clearly agreed with the general proposition that healthcare has always fallen under the purview of elite power by various forms of legislative favour. While 40 per cent of those surveyed disagreed with the statement, 50 per cent expressed a positive or sympathetic response. That said, a significant minority of respondents – some 10 per cent – confessed to not having thought about healthcare in terms of societal and elite power.

Conclusion

One result is clear. There is no consensus behind the NHS – though there is no consensus behind a completely market-oriented system of health provision either. With regard to the possibility of monopoly, respondents were more strongly against state monopoly than they were against the private sector. Though a small minority would favour a completely market-oriented system, the answers of most respondents seem to implicitly accept the neoclassical model of market failure in proposing government intervention in areas where neoclassical models are said to identify weaknesses in markets. Despite this, the respondents clearly recognised the potential for government failure. For example, while seeming to accept the problem of information asymmetry in markets, the opinion formers clearly expressed concerns about the withholding of information by governments. The same is true, for example, with regard to problems such as moral hazard. Both private insurance markets and taxpayer-funded systems were thought to be subject to such problems.

There is no general acceptance of a free market in healthcare – or necessarily a clear understanding of what a market in healthcare would entail. At the same time, the utopian vision of state-run systems has evaporated – especially among those not part of the political system – and the advantages of markets over state provision, in many respects are understood.

8 A RADICAL VISION OF MARKETS IN HEALTHCARE

Introduction

The results of the previous chapter emphasise the need for those who believe in markets for health to package their arguments differently – avoiding, where possible, the neoclassical framework which invites the response of market failure analysis. Market failure analysis highlights problems such as social costs and benefits or externalities. Economists argue that if the government can intervene and bring private costs and benefits into line with true social costs and benefits, the exchanges that occur will be more socially beneficial. For them, government intervention can be easily justified. Different arguments for government intervention are proposed to deal with public goods, asymmetric information and transactions costs.

An externality occurs when, as Tyler Cowen has put it: '… one person's actions affect another person's well-being and the relevant costs and benefits are not reflected in market prices'.[1] Externalities therefore cause net social benefit to diverge from net private benefit. It is important to recognise, however, that in arguing that private net benefit sometimes differs from social net benefit does not automatically justify government intervention.

1   Tyler Cowen, 'Public goods and externalities', Library of Economics and Liberty, online at: www.econlib.org/library/Enc/PublicGoodsandExternalities.html.

For, as Cowen also points out: 'The imperfections of market solutions to public goods problems must be weighed against the imperfections of government solutions. Governments rely on bureaucracy and have weak incentives to serve consumers. Therefore, they produce inefficiently.'[2] Indeed, there is no reason to suppose that governments can accurately identify and quantify the level of the externality – never mind develop and implement the optimal policy to deal with the problem.

It is also the case that opponents of a market in healthcare attack a caricature of the market. In particular, they often attack the high costs of the US system, which are, arguably, the result of government intervention in a system that is both highly regulated, subject to state-sanctioned monopolies and, in large part, has healthcare both financed and provided by the state. We now draw out the implications of a fully private market in health finance and provision.

Towards a market in healthcare

Critically analysing notions of market failure in health systems, Hans-Hermann Hoppe[3] wrote a paper entitled 'A four-step health-care solution'.[4] Arguing that the American healthcare system is

---

2   Ibid.

3   For Hoppe's main works, see H. Hoppe, *Democracy: The God that Failed*, Trans-action, New Brunswick, NJ, 2002; *Economic Science and the Austrian Method*, Ludwig von Mises Institute, Auburn, AL, 1995; *The Economics and Ethics of Private Property: Studies in Political Economy and Philosophy*, Kluwer Academic Publishers, Boston, MA, 1993; *A Theory of Socialism and Capitalism: Economics, Politics and Ethics*, Kluwer Academic Publishers, Boston, MA, 1989; *The Myth of National Defense: Essays in the Theory and History of Security Production* (ed.), Ludwig von Mises Institute, Auburn, AL, 2002.

4   Hans-Hermann Hoppe, 'A four-step health-care solution', *The Free Market*, 11(4),

'a mess'[5] and that 'this demonstrates not market but government failure',[6] he commences by asserting:

> To cure the problem requires not different or more government regulations and bureaucracies, as self-serving politicians want us to believe, but the elimination of all existing government controls … It's time to get serious about health care reform. Tax credits, vouchers, and privatisation will go a long way towards decentralizing the system and removing unnecessary burdens from business. But four additional steps must also be taken.[7]

For Hoppe, point one requires the abandonment of state regulatory controls and market interventions in favour of a pure market driven by reputation and meaningful competition. He suggests eliminating:

> … all licensing requirements for medical schools, hospitals, pharmacies, and medical doctors and other health care personnel … a greater variety of health care services would appear on the market … Competing voluntary accreditation agencies would take the place of compulsory government licensing … Because consumers would no longer be duped into believing that there is such a thing as a 'national standard' of health care, they will increase their search costs and make more discriminating health care choices.[8]

Point two demands that the state completely withdraws from pharmaceuticals and medical devices. He proposes the elimination of:

Ludwig von Mises Institute, Auburn, AL, April 1993.

5   Ibid., p. 1.
6   Ibid.
7   Ibid.
8   Ibid.

… all government restrictions on the production and sale of pharmaceutical products and medical devices … Costs and prices would fall, and a wider variety of better products would reach the market sooner. The market would force consumers to act in accordance with their own – rather than the government's – risk assessment. And competing drug and device manufacturers and sellers, to safeguard against product liability suits as much as to attract customers, would provide increasingly better product descriptions and guarantees.[9]

Hoppe continues with point three, which asserts that government should completely deregulate and open up to real consumer choices the private medical insurance market. He does not regard insurance as the only answer, however – especially where people can determine their own health outcomes. He says:

Deregulate the health insurance industry. Private enterprise can offer insurance against events over whose outcome the insured possesses no control. One cannot insure oneself against suicide or bankruptcy, for example, because it is in one's own hands to bring these events about … Because a person's health, or lack of it, lies increasingly within his own control, many, if not most health risks, are actually uninsurable. 'Insurance' against risks whose likelihood an individual can systematically influence falls within that person's own responsibility.[10]

He continues:

I would not want to pool my personal accident risks with those of professional football players, for instance, but

9   Ibid.
10   Ibid., pp. 1–2.

exclusively with those people in circumstances similar to my own, at lower costs.[11]

In other words, he argues that differential premiums that are commensurate with the risks that people willingly take on in their lives are important.

In attacking the damaging failings of legislative favour in American health insurance, Hoppe also highlights the distortions that lie behind this most corporatist and politicised of sectors – often caricatured by British proponents of the NHS as a free market. He argues that:

> To deregulate the industry means to restore it to unrestricted freedom of contract. Uninsurable risks would lose coverage, the variety of insurance policies for the remaining coverage would increase, and price differentials would reflect genuine insurance risks. On average, prices would drastically fall. And the reform would restore individual responsibility in health care.[12]

Finally, Hoppe argues for the denationalisation of health and welfare funding in an attempt to guard against the moral hazards associated with government resources, including the abolition of Medicare and Medicaid.

At the end of Hoppe's analysis and promotion of a real market in medicine and healthcare he asserts that: 'Only these four steps, although drastic, will restore a fully free market in medical provision. Until they are adopted, the industry will have serious problems, and so will we, its customers.'[13]

---

11 Ibid., p. 2.
12 Ibid.
13 Ibid.

The bankrupt market failure doctrine

For David Friedman, the leading anarcho-capitalist and author of *The Machinery of Freedom*,[14] goods and services are produced and allocated in several different ways. In addition to the market there is household production, which is the way in which children are reared, homes cleaned, clothes washed and most meals cooked. There is also political production.[15]

While household production represents a substantial fraction of the economy (for example, parents serving as nurses for their sick children, grown children taking care of ageing parents), Friedman's work is primarily concerned with production and allocation via the market versus production and allocation by government. The main question he tries to answer is whether one form of production should be preferred and if so which? In his 'Should medicine be a commodity?', Friedman comments:

> Economic efficiency is a strong requirement for the outcome of any real world system of institutions, since an outcome is efficient only if it could not be improved by a bureaucrat god – a benevolent despot with perfect information and unlimited power over individual actions. While it may be seen as an upper bound on how well an economic system can work, one might think that using that bound to judge real systems is as appropriate as judging race cars by their ability to achieve their upper bound – the speed of light.[16]

---

14 David Friedman, *The Machinery of Freedom: A Guide to Radical Capitalism*, Open Court Publishing, Chicago, IL, 1978.

15 Friedman speculates that it is even not clear that the market represents a larger part of the total economy than alternative ways.

16 David Friedman, 'Should medicine be a commodity?', published online at: www.daviddfriedman.com/Academic/Medicine_Commodity/Medicine_Commodity.html. See p. 7.

For Friedman, it is one thing to show that there is something a government could do in theory that would improve on the outcome of the unregulated market and another entirely different and much more difficult matter to show that what government is actually able to do would improve upon the market outcome:

> That would require a theory of governmental behaviour comparable in power and precision to the theory of market behaviour from which the original efficiency theorem and the inefficiencies due to failures of its assumptions were derived. No widely accepted theory of that sort exists, and much of the large and growing literature that attempts to produce such a theory seems to suggest that government intervention is more likely to worsen than to improve market outcomes.[17]

He suggests that the best analysis available is 'public choice': or the economics of the political market. Public choice theory attempts to analyse the political system by using the same approach by which ordinary economics analyses the private market. Crucially, it applies the techniques of economic analysis (monopoly, competition, information costs) to political and bureaucratic behaviour. It drops the traditional assumption that politicians and bureaucrats try to serve only 'the public interest' and more realistically assumes that, as elsewhere, they try to serve their own interests by re-election and empire-building. The vote motive in politics is akin to the profit motive in industry.[18]

The important question, however, is not whether the political

17 Ibid., p. 8.
18 Gordon Tullock, *The Vote Motive*, Institute of Economic Affairs, London, 2006; James Buchanan, 'The development of public choice', in *The Economics of Politics*, Institute of Economic Affairs, London, 1978; James Buchanan and Gordon Tullock, *The Calculus of Consent*, University of Michigan Press, 1962.

market works under conditions of zero transaction costs and perfect information. Under those assumptions the private market is also perfectly efficient. The really interesting question is how badly each system breaks down when the assumptions are relaxed. Countering the claim that 'health is too important to be left to the market',[19] Friedman retorts: 'My response would be that the market is, generally speaking, the best set of institutions we know of for producing and distributing things. The more important the good is, the stronger the argument for having it produced by the market.'[20]

In Britain, Friedman's perspective is echoed in the writings of Brian Micklethwait. Like Friedman, Micklethwait describes himself as an anarcho-capitalist.[21] Whereas in Britain mainstream health economists have traditionally emphasised the particular, unique nature of healthcare, however, arguing that market failure is a real concern to be checked by government, Micklethwait comments: 'Medicine is often described as special, and it is special. But so are all businesses. Every kind of business has its own unique features which make it unlike any other business. But that doesn't mean that it should not be a business … '[22]

Perhaps the most widely read free market health policy expert in Britain is Dr David Green, director of Civitas. He has long championed the debunking of three types of market failure ideas in modern health economics.

Green argues that professional monopoly power is not inherent in healthcare, but arises because governments either

19 Friedman, 'Should medicine be a commodity?', op. cit., p. 42.

20 Ibid.

21 Brian Micklethwait, *Why I Call Myself a Free Market Anarchist and Why I Am One*, Political Notes no. 67, Libertarian Alliance, London, 1992.

22 Brian Micklethwait in conversation with the author in 2005.

actively or passively accept it. Professional bodies can exert considerable control when they are seeking the grant and perpetuation of legislative favour.

Concerning notions of consumer ignorance, Green argues that there is an asymmetry of knowledge in any market where people are paying for the expertise of others – for example, lawyers, mechanics and accountants. But he points out that this does not preclude the operation of a viable and sustainable market that is better than alternative forms of economic organisation. Instead, much of the uncertainty faced in healthcare, particularly in terms of outcomes, exists for clinicians as much as for patients. He also observes that consumer ignorance may, in major measure, be due to the highly restrictive practices of health professionals, particularly when it comes to health information, advertising and sharing knowledge with patients on issues of access to alternative options.

Concerning the issue of moral hazard, Green points out that, in Britain, healthcare is in large measure provided by the public sector and therefore heavily subsidised by the taxpayer. The public sector patient is therefore in the same position as an insured private patient to the extent that payment at the point of service understates the true cost of supplying the service. For Green, this reality means that inflated demand will occur in either sector and that problems of moral hazard inevitably arise in both state and market systems.

The idea that government is in some way a superior agent, however, over and above a spontaneous and free market, is increasingly being rejected. For Hoppe, Friedman, Green and Micklethwait the very idea of market failure is itself dubious, because it imputes upon the market a status of 'absolute perfectionism' that its defenders would never want to claim. To these writers, health economics can never be addressed in such fixed and absolutist terms as 'failure' or 'success'. Instead, they believe the market is better and more accurately viewed as a superior process of discovery and of trial and error to that which government allocation of resources could achieve.

Friedman argues that the notion of market failure in health economics and its popularity with most opinion formers has arisen because most people '… interpret the problem in terms of fairness rather than efficiency'.[23]

Commenting on those people who often unconsciously adhere to commonly held notions of market failure in health, he asserts:

> … they may be making the error of judging a system by the comparison between its outcome and the best outcome that can be described, rather than judging it by a comparison between its outcome and the outcome that would actually be produced by the best alternative system available. If, as seems likely, all possible sets of institutions fall short of producing perfect outcomes, then a policy of comparing observed outcomes to ideal ones will reject any existing system.[24]

In examining the psychology of the health policy debate and the negative attitude that many people have towards the market, Friedman concludes that exactly the same concerns can be expressed when it comes to government intervention. 'It is easy, and satisfying,' he argues, 'to pick some unattractive outcome – a poor man, actual or imaginary, turned away from the expensive private hospital that could have cured his disease – and describe it

---

23   Friedman, 'Should medicine be a commodity?', op. cit., p. 42.
24   Ibid.

as "intolerable," "unacceptable," or some similar epithet designed to prevent further discussion.'[25]

Friedman points out, however, that the same game can be applied with reference to the public sector: 'In a large and complicated society, it is likely that any system for producing and allocating medical care – or doing anything else difficult and important – will sometimes produce outcomes that can plausibly be labelled as intolerable.'[26]

Warning against the political and economic psychology of market failure, Friedman powerfully concludes: 'The question we should ask, and try to answer, is not what outcome would be ideal but what outcome we can expect from each of various alternative sets of institutions, and which, from that limited set of alternatives, we prefer.'[27]

Friedman himself concludes that there is no good reason to expect that government involvement in the medical market produces more desirable results than a market would.

25   Ibid., p. 43.
26   Ibid., p. 43.
27   Ibid.

9 FROM GOVERNMENT FAILURE TO A FREE MARKET?

Introduction

This monograph has examined notions of government and market failure in British healthcare by tracking and analysing the changing views of opinion formers. In presenting the research findings I have highlighted the attitudes of today's opinion formers towards populist notions of health economics and provided insights into the limits and boundaries of contemporary debate. We begin this chapter by summarising our earlier findings. We then examine how the boundaries of the debate can be pushed farther.

The current boundaries of debate

Significantly, our findings have shown that substantial swathes of elite opinion no longer support the National Health Service (NHS) in its traditional fully nationalised form. Instead, a majority of opinion formers now believe in a much greater role for private healthcare, although they remain sceptical of a genuinely liberal position, particularly in the case of those who work in the political system. Overall, the following pattern emerges.

Looking at private funding arrangements verses the state, a majority of the opinion formers surveyed believe that because people's healthcare is unpredictable, some of its costs will always have to be covered by private healthcare – 'government arrangements such as taxation cannot do it all'. Perhaps mindful of the pressures on the NHS and contributions made by a wide range of health and social care charities, most respondents believe that the state cannot cover the costs of unlimited healthcare.

That said, the average respondent also believes that if a real market in healthcare existed government would still have to intervene to protect the poor and chronically sick from neglect. Indeed, the opinion formers believe that many of the points that can be made against state healthcare can also made against private healthcare. Recognising the inevitability of scarce resources, both systems are thought to be 'inequitable', 'two tier', 'rationed' and 'costly'.

Similarly, many of the positive points concerning private healthcare are also used to support state involvement. Both, in certain ways, are seen as being potentially 'efficient', 'helping the poor to do better' and ultimately 'cost effective'. That said, while the average respondent sees full-blown state healthcare as being 'utopian', 'bureaucratic' and requiring 'higher taxes', the market is generally thought superior at harnessing 'innovation', providing 'better information' and encouraging 'greater personal responsibility'.

Significantly, the average respondent tends to favour public–private partnerships but does not equate the concept of monopoly with the monopoly power of the medical and other healthcare professions. Indeed, very few respondents seem to appreciate that healthcare, irrespective of sector, is ultimately predicated upon the legislative favour granted by government to the professions.

Most respondents tend to believe that if a system of real state healthcare existed, a market providing people with choices would still have to be allowed to prevent problems of monopoly. Echoing the principles of libertarian orthodoxy, they tend to see state healthcare as being a much greater monopolist than the market.

Most opinion formers support the view that if a system of complete state monopoly healthcare existed, people would have to be allowed access to a wide range of competing health information sources to help them overcome the problems of consumer ignorance. Wary of the state control of information, a majority side with the principles of the open society and reject state censorship.

Again, sensitive and hostile to governmental cost containment measures, respondents identify Treasury ministers and medical professionals as benefiting from the statutory restrictions on the advertising of medicines.

The average respondent believes that if a real market in healthcare existed, government would still have to intervene to help protect people from such external factors as contagious disease. At the same time, however, they tend not to trust politicians and government to be 'open from the start and to do the right things'. On this latter point, 'cock-up' tends to be most opinion formers preferred view of government failure, not conspiracy.

In response to the statement 'Many people argue that because disease and epidemics can impact on everyone in society, politicians must be in charge of public health', the average respondent accepted the role for politicians and/or the state but they tended to add the caveat that other experts, such as clinicians, should be fully involved. Provided medical, health and security professionals have an appropriate input, few respondents object to politicians and the state intervening in times of epidemic or national emergency. More generally, the average respondent viewed healthcare as being a natural private good – not a public good as often argued in many academic textbooks.

Respondents also tended to believe that the problem of moral hazard, often cited as a form of 'market failure', was also prevalent in the public sector. Thus state healthcare was viewed as providing perverse incentives to over-consume at additional cost to the taxpayer. This finding, once again, illustrates the irrelevance of the market failure paradigm in that it appears that it is not possible for the government to correct what is often termed as a failure of the market.

Finally, the average opinion former tends to be uncertain when it comes to the idea that through the granting of legislative favour, the state has always sought to empire-build and to control people's access to healthcare and medicine. There is a general belief that history is more complex than this – although there is also a willingness to accept that the NHS benefits the middle classes more than the poorest and most disadvantaged in society.

How the boundaries of debate are changing

Overall, these results show that the world has moved on significantly since the heady days of the 1940s – and perhaps even since the 1980s, when the NHS monopoly remained unchallenged among the political class. Today, there is not only greater understanding of the failure of state healthcare – and a more balanced approach towards the appropriate role of markets – but also an awareness of the problems of producer capture.

In its traditional, fully nationalised mode the NHS enjoys little support among opinion formers, who have much less faith in the authority of top-down direction than previous generations and show a clear acceptance of markets and a key role for consumers.

That being said, while the overall debate remains dominated

by corporatist notions of public–private partnerships, there is as yet only marginal support for a genuine libertarian market in healthcare and full-blown professional demonopolisation.

Today, as with most other historic phases in the development of medicine and healthcare, the overwhelming majority of opinion formers believe that there is an important role (however loosely defined) for government.

It is clear from the results that the state is still seen by opinion formers to be the ultimate guarantor of communitarian safety. It is also seen as a vital institutional nexus responsible for the setting of professional standards and the enforcement of contracts. That said, there is a much greater awareness of the dangers of professional, monopoly and producer capture than was the case when the NHS was formed.

In the contemporary healthcare debate, while the utopian statism of the early NHS now finds little favour, the more fundamental rubrics legitimising state intervention remain. Not only do the limits and boundaries of contemporary policy conversation recognise a role for state intervention but, as with defence, intelligence and policing, healthcare is viewed as an integral part of an essentially statist order.

Pushing the boundaries farther

However strident and popular ideas of market-driven healthcare might become in the years ahead there are, as yet, few opinion formers who truly question the grander and statist narrative underpinning the discourse of healthcare and its professionals.

As with the healthcare systems that flourished during the Middle Ages and the nineteenth century, the ultimate rubrics of statism remain largely unchallenged in their institutional and moral senses. However powerful free-market consumerism might become in the future, a residual acceptance of state power provides the intellectual platform upon which legislative favour can be inexorably sought and no doubt perpetuated.

In many ways healthcare has always been a deeply corporatist venture run in association with a range of mystical, military, religious or purely political state elites: the forces Ayn Rand has so powerfully characterised as the witch doctor and Attila.[1] Yet, as in all previous eras, politics, state coercion and power not only seem set to remain entwined with the affairs of healthcare, but the modern biomedical paradigm appears to be firmly bound by its political and economic discourse and constraints.

In the years ahead, as opinion formers continue to gradually accept ever greater roles for independent healthcare, one is therefore unlikely to hear demands for a truly radical shake-up of healthcare even from the private sector itself. Instead, all the indications suggest that most mainstream players in British healthcare will continue to prefer gradual and incremental reform. Mindful of their short-term interests and peers, they will shun the competitive dynamism and successes of a genuine market in favour of a more limited and conservative approach.

Thus, to challenge such institutional inertia and pull the debate farther in the direction of the market, it is vital that libertarian doctors and nurses stand up and campaign for substantive change in the years ahead. That is why free market think tanks and groups such as Nurses for Reform (NFR) are so important. It is notable that think tanks, academics and political advisers (who have often

---

1   Ayn Rand, *For the New Intellectual: The Philosophy of Ayn Rand*, Random House, New York, 1961.

worked in think tanks or as academics) tended to have the most pro-market views in our survey. Indeed, it is not only notable but significant. Opinion in the institutions of government, the media and so on is often led by academics and also by opinion formers in think tanks. The policy ideas of the latter, who work to make ideas that are academically respectable comprehensible in policy circles, often lead actual policy developments by several years.

To continue to help opinion formers and the public accept free markets in healthcare it is vital that state failure is systematically exposed at every turn, so as to balance the focus that often appears on market failure. We need also to intellectually, morally and culturally challenge professional monopoly practices. Healthcare delivery should be returned to an independent sector that includes a diverse range of for-profit and not-for-profit providers. Politicians should be pressurised to end their historic obsession with the idea of state provision and embrace the independent sector, even if this means offering ownership of NHS hospitals and clinics on a cooperative basis to the people who actually work in and run them.

The General Medical Council and Nursing and Midwifery Council should not be allowed to be professional monopolists – instead, they should be trusted Kitemarks. The British Medical Association and the Royal College of Nursing should lose their monopoly status in law and instead operate in a competitive and open market. The next government should face down these middle-class trade unions, erecting endless roadblocks on the way to genuine consumer empowerment and choice, just as Margaret Thatcher dealt with their blue-collar equivalents in the 1980s. It goes without saying that national collective pay bargaining should be abandoned at the earliest possible opportunity.

Similarly, the next government should take clear steps to end health censorship. In today's Internet age it is absurd that open advertising by doctors, nurses, hospitals, clinics and pharmaceutical companies is still largely restricted or subject to outright bans. The next government must accept that only better-informed people will be able to take better and more responsible decisions. While there is no such thing as perfect information or knowledge, advertising and the building of powerful brands will nevertheless help to deliver powerful checks against the conservative forces of producer capture and consumer ignorance.

In opening up all health provision to the independent sector, actively demonopolising the medical and healthcare professions, and ending healthcare censorship, British healthcare will finally start to implement the supply-side reforms that it so desperately requires.

To complete the process, however, it is vital that the Treasury also complements these reforms by not standing in the way of a private funding revolution. Any incoming administration should find ways of making it advantageous for people to offer and take out existing and new forms of independent health funding, including health savings accounts and cash top-ups. The best way to do this is to dramatically lower taxes and to deregulate the insurance and financial products market. Significantly, trade unions, friendly societies, churches and charities must all be freed up to play their rightful part in a new and dynamic market that genuinely puts patients, the poor and the mentally ill first.

Today, too many nursing and medical trade unions fail the professionals they purport to protect because they invariably stick to old and outdated agendas. Instead of championing substantive reform – and in so doing, championing the rights of patients as genuine consumers – they default to comment on specific short-term issues such as demanding more taxpayers' money or new forms of legislative favour. Such an approach is not only disastrous for the professionals involved but also for patients and those in genuine need.

Indeed, what the research at the heart of this study has demonstrated is that not only has the world changed in important and significant ways but, while many of the above policy recommendations would have been derided only a quarter of a century ago, in 2008 they are perceived to be at the cutting edge of debate. Today, a majority of those surveyed believe that healthcare is a natural private good and that taxation can no longer 'do it all'. They associate the market with innovation and greater personal responsibility. Crucially, there is a growing and shared understanding that the NHS benefits the middle classes more than the poorest and most disadvantaged in society.

Finally, in the 60th anniversary year of the NHS, a majority of health opinion formers no longer support nationalisation. Instead they openly believe in a much greater role for private healthcare. In 2008, it is time to recognise state failure in healthcare and to embrace genuine markets.

ABOUT THE IEA

The Institute is a research and educational charity (No. CC 235 351), limited by guarantee. Its mission is to improve understanding of the fundamental institutions of a free society by analysing and expounding the role of markets in solving economic and social problems.

The IEA achieves its mission by:

- a high-quality publishing programme
- conferences, seminars, lectures and other events
- outreach to school and college students
- brokering media introductions and appearances

The IEA, which was established in 1955 by the late Sir Antony Fisher, is an educational charity, not a political organisation. It is independent of any political party or group and does not carry on activities intended to affect support for any political party or candidate in any election or referendum, or at any other time. It is financed by sales of publications, conference fees and voluntary donations.

In addition to its main series of publications the IEA also publishes a quarterly journal, *Economic Affairs*.

The IEA is aided in its work by a distinguished international Academic Advisory Council and an eminent panel of Honorary Fellows. Together with other academics, they review prospective IEA publications, their comments being passed on anonymously to authors. All IEA papers are therefore subject to the same rigorous independent refereeing process as used by leading academic journals.

IEA publications enjoy widespread classroom use and course adoptions in schools and universities. They are also sold throughout the world and often translated/reprinted.

Since 1974 the IEA has helped to create a worldwide network of 100 similar institutions in over 70 countries. They are all independent but share the IEA's mission.

Views expressed in the IEA's publications are those of the authors, not those of the Institute (which has no corporate view), its Managing Trustees, Academic Advisory Council members or senior staff.

Members of the Institute's Academic Advisory Council, Honorary Fellows, Trustees and Staff are listed on the following page.

The Institute gratefully acknowledges financial support for its publications programme and other work from a generous benefaction by the late Alec and Beryl Warren.

The Institute of Economic Affairs
2 Lord North Street, Westminster, London SW1P 3LB
Tel: 020 7799 8900
Fax: 020 7799 2137
Email: iea@iea.org.uk
Internet: iea.org.uk

165

Other papers recently published by the IEA include:

WHO, What and Why?
Transnational Government, Legitimacy and the World Health Organization
Roger Scruton
Occasional Paper 113; ISBN 0 255 36487 3; £8.00

The World Turned Rightside Up
A New Trading Agenda for the Age of Globalisation
John C. Hulsman
Occasional Paper 114; ISBN 0 255 36495 4; £8.00

The Representation of Business in English Literature
Introduced and edited by Arthur Pollard
Readings 53; ISBN 0 255 36491 1; £12.00

Anti-Liberalism 2000
The Rise of New Millennium Collectivism
David Henderson
Occasional Paper 115; ISBN 0 255 36497 0; £7.50

Capitalism, Morality and Markets
Brian Griffiths, Robert A. Sirico, Norman Barry & Frank Field
Readings 54; ISBN 0 255 36496 2; £7.50

A Conversation with Harris and Seldon
Ralph Harris & Arthur Seldon
Occasional Paper 116; ISBN 0 255 36498 9; £7.50

Malaria and the DDT Story
Richard Tren & Roger Bate
Occasional Paper 117; ISBN 0 255 36499 7; £10.00

A Plea to Economists Who Favour Liberty: Assist the Everyman
Daniel B. Klein
Occasional Paper 118; ISBN 0 255 36501 2; £10.00

The Changing Fortunes of Economic Liberalism
Yesterday, Today and Tomorrow
David Henderson
Occasional Paper 105 (new edition); ISBN 0 255 36520 9; £12.50

The Global Education Industry
Lessons from Private Education in Developing Countries
James Tooley
Hobart Paper 141 (new edition); ISBN 0 255 36503 9; £12.50

Saving Our Streams
*The Role of the Anglers' Conservation Association in
Protecting English and Welsh Rivers*
Roger Bate
Research Monograph 53; ISBN 0 255 36494 6; £10.00

Better Off Out?
The Benefits or Costs of EU Membership
Brian Hindley & Martin Howe
Occasional Paper 99 (new edition); ISBN 0 255 36502 0; £10.00

Buckingham at 25
Freeing the Universities from State Control
Edited by James Tooley
Readings 55; ISBN 0 255 36512 8; £15.00

Lectures on Regulatory and Competition Policy
Irwin M. Stelzer
Occasional Paper 120; ISBN 0 255 36511 X; £12.50

Misguided Virtue
False Notions of Corporate Social Responsibility
David Henderson
Hobart Paper 142; ISBN 0 255 36510 1; £12.50

Should We Have Faith in Central Banks?
Otmar Issing
Occasional Paper 125; ISBN 0 255 36528 4; £7.50

The Dilemma of Democracy
Arthur Seldon
Hobart Paper 136 (reissue); ISBN 0 255 36536 5; £10.00

Capital Controls: a 'Cure' Worse Than the Problem?
Forrest Capie
Research Monograph 56; ISBN 0 255 36506 3; £10.00

The Poverty of 'Development Economics'
Deepak Lal
Hobart Paper 144 (reissue); ISBN 0 255 36519 5; £15.00

Should Britain Join the Euro?
The Chancellor's Five Tests Examined
Patrick Minford
Occasional Paper 126; ISBN 0 255 36527 6; £7.50

Post-Communist Transition: Some Lessons
Leszek Balcerowicz
Occasional Paper 127; ISBN 0 255 36533 0; £7.50

A Tribute to Peter Bauer
John Blundell et al.
Occasional Paper 128; ISBN 0 255 36531 4; £10.00

Employment Tribunals
Their Growth and the Case for Radical Reform
J. R. Shackleton
Hobart Paper 145; ISBN 0 255 36515 2; £10.00

Fifty Economic Fallacies Exposed
Geoffrey E. Wood
Occasional Paper 129; ISBN 0 255 36518 7; £12.50

A Market in Airport Slots

Keith Boyfield (editor), David Starkie, Tom Bass & Barry Humphreys
Readings 56; ISBN 0 255 36505 5; £10.00

Money, Inflation and the Constitutional Position of the Central Bank

Milton Friedman & Charles A. E. Goodhart
Readings 57; ISBN 0 255 36538 1; £10.00

railway.com

Parallels between the Early British Railways and the ICT Revolution
Robert C. B. Miller
Research Monograph 57; ISBN 0 255 36534 9; £12.50

The Regulation of Financial Markets

Edited by Philip Booth & David Currie
Readings 58; ISBN 0 255 36551 9; £12.50

Climate Alarmism Reconsidered

Robert L. Bradley Jr
Hobart Paper 146; ISBN 0 255 36541 1; £12.50

Government Failure: E. G. West on Education

Edited by James Tooley & James Stanfield
Occasional Paper 130; ISBN 0 255 36552 7; £12.50

Corporate Governance: Accountability in the Marketplace

Elaine Sternberg
Second edition
Hobart Paper 147; ISBN 0 255 36542 x; £12.50

The Land Use Planning System

Evaluating Options for Reform
John Corkindale
Hobart Paper 148; ISBN 0 255 36550 0; £10.00

Economy and Virtue
Essays on the Theme of Markets and Morality
Edited by Dennis O'Keeffe
Readings 59; ISBN 0 255 36504 7; £12.50

Free Markets Under Siege
Cartels, Politics and Social Welfare
Richard A. Epstein
Occasional Paper 132; ISBN 0 255 36553 5; £10.00

Unshackling Accountants
D. R. Myddelton
Hobart Paper 149; ISBN 0 255 36559 4; £12.50

The Euro as Politics
Pedro Schwartz
Research Monograph 58; ISBN 0 255 36535 7; £12.50

Pricing Our Roads
Vision and Reality
Stephen Glaister & Daniel J. Graham
Research Monograph 59; ISBN 0 255 36562 4; £10.00

The Role of Business in the Modern World
Progress, Pressures, and Prospects for the Market Economy
David Henderson
Hobart Paper 150; ISBN 0 255 36548 9; £12.50

Public Service Broadcasting Without the BBC?
Alan Peacock
Occasional Paper 133; ISBN 0 255 36565 9; £10.00

The ECB and the Euro: the First Five Years
Otmar Issing
Occasional Paper 134; ISBN 0 255 36555 1; £10.00

Towards a Liberal Utopia?
Edited by Philip Booth
Hobart Paperback 32; ISBN 0 255 36563 2; £15.00

The Way Out of the Pensions Quagmire
Philip Booth & Deborah Cooper
Research Monograph 60; ISBN 0 255 36517 9; £12.50

Black Wednesday
A Re-examination of Britain's Experience in the Exchange Rate Mechanism
Alan Budd
Occasional Paper 135; ISBN 0 255 36566 7; £7.50

Crime: Economic Incentives and Social Networks
Paul Ormerod
Hobart Paper 151; ISBN 0 255 36554 3; £10.00

The Road to Serfdom *with* **The Intellectuals and Socialism**
Friedrich A. Hayek
Occasional Paper 136; ISBN 0 255 36576 4; £10.00

Money and Asset Prices in Boom and Bust
Tim Congdon
Hobart Paper 152; ISBN 0 255 36570 5; £10.00

The Dangers of Bus Re-regulation
and Other Perspectives on Markets in Transport
John Hibbs et al.
Occasional Paper 137; ISBN 0 255 36572 1; £10.00

The New Rural Economy
Change, Dynamism and Government Policy
Berkeley Hill et al.
Occasional Paper 138; ISBN 0 255 36546 2; £15.00

The Benefits of Tax Competition
Richard Teather
Hobart Paper 153; ISBN 0 255 36569 1; £12.50

Wheels of Fortune
Self-funding Infrastructure and the Free Market Case for a Land Tax
Fred Harrison
Hobart Paper 154; ISBN 0 255 36589 6; £12.50

Were 364 Economists All Wrong?
Edited by Philip Booth
Readings 60; ISBN 978 0 255 36588 8; £10.00

Europe After the 'No' Votes
Mapping a New Economic Path
Patrick A. Messerlin
Occasional Paper 139; ISBN 978 0 255 36580 2; £10.00

The Railways, the Market and the Government
John Hibbs et al.
Readings 61; ISBN 978 0 255 36567 3; £12.50

Corruption: The World's Big C
Cases, Causes, Consequences, Cures
Ian Senior
Research Monograph 61; ISBN 978 0 255 36571 0; £12.50

Choice and the End of Social Housing
Peter King
Hobart Paper 155; ISBN 978 0 255 36568 0; £10.00

Sir Humphrey's Legacy
Facing Up to the Cost of Public Sector Pensions
Neil Record
Hobart Paper 156; ISBN 978 0 255 36578 9; £10.00

The Economics of Law
Cento Veljanovski
Second edition
Hobart Paper 157; ISBN 978 0 255 36561 1; £12.50

Living with Leviathan
Public Spending, Taxes and Economic Performance
David B. Smith
Hobart Paper 158; ISBN 978 0 255 36579 6; £12.50

The Vote Motive
Gordon Tullock
New edition
Hobart Paperback 33; ISBN 978 0 255 36577 2; £10.00

Waging the War of Ideas
John Blundell
Third edition
Occasional Paper 131; ISBN 978 0 255 36606 9; £12.50

The War Between the State and the Family
How Government Divides and Impoverishes
Patricia Morgan
Hobart Paper 159; ISBN 978 0 255 36596 3; £10.00

Capitalism – A Condensed Version
Arthur Seldon
Occasional Paper 140; ISBN 978 0 255 36598 7; £7.50

Catholic Social Teaching and the Market Economy
Edited by Philip Booth
Hobart Paperback 34; ISBN 978 0 255 36581 9; £15.00

Adam Smith – A Primer
Eamonn Butler
Occasional Paper 141; ISBN 978 0 255 36608 3; £7.50

Happiness, Economics and Public Policy
Helen Johns & Paul Ormerod
Research Monograph 62; ISBN 978 0 255 36600 7; £10.00

They Meant Well
Government Project Disasters
D. R. Myddelton
Hobart Paper 160; ISBN 978 0 255 36601 4; £12.50

Rescuing Social Capital from Social Democracy
John Meadowcroft & Mark Pennington
Hobart Paper 161; ISBN 978 0 255 36592 5; £10.00

Paths to Property
Approaches to Institutional Change in International Development
Karol Boudreaux & Paul Dragos Aligica
Hobart Paper 162; ISBN 978 0 255 36582 6; £10.00

Prohibitions
Edited by John Meadowcroft
Hobart Paperback 35; ISBN 978 0 255 36585 7; £15.00

Trade Policy, New Century
The WTO, FTAs and Asia Rising
Razeen Sally
Hobart Paper 163; ISBN 978 0 255 36544 4; £12.50

Other IEA publications

Comprehensive information on other publications and the wider work of the IEA can be found at www.iea.org.uk. To order any publication please see below.

Personal customers

Orders from personal customers should be directed to the IEA:
Bob Layson
IEA
2 Lord North Street
FREEPOST LON10168
London SW1P 3YZ
Tel: 020 7799 8909. Fax: 020 7799 2137
Email: blayson@iea.org.uk

Trade customers

All orders from the book trade should be directed to the IEA's distributor:
Gazelle Book Services Ltd (IEA Orders)
FREEPOST RLYS-EAHU-YSCZ
White Cross Mills
Hightown
Lancaster LA1 4XS
Tel: 01524 68765, Fax: 01524 53232
Email: sales@gazellebooks.co.uk

IEA subscriptions

The IEA also offers a subscription service to its publications. For a single annual payment (currently £42.00 in the UK), subscribers receive every monograph the IEA publishes. For more information please contact:
Adam Myers
Subscriptions
IEA
2 Lord North Street
FREEPOST LON10168
London SW1P 3YZ
Tel: 020 7799 8920, Fax: 020 7799 2137
Email: amyers@iea.org.uk